D1220680

PEOPLES
of
WESTERN ASIA

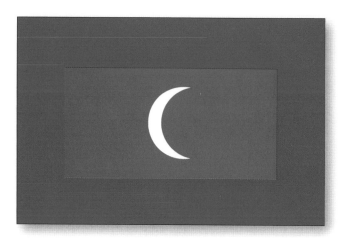

Maldives

Oman

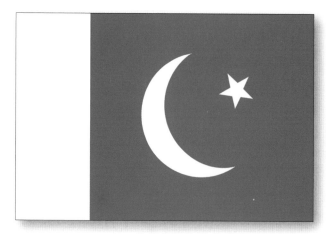

Pakistan

PEOPLES
of
WESTERN ASIA

Volume 6
Maldives–Pakistan

Marshall Cavendish
Reference
New York

Marshall Cavendish Corporation
99 White Plains Road
Tarrytown, New York 10591

www.marshallcavendish.us

©2007 Marshall Cavendish Corporation

Consultant:
   Morris Rossabi, Professor and Senior Research Scholar,
      Columbia University

Contributing authors:
   Fiona Macdonald
   Esther Raizen
   Gillian Stacey
   Philip Steele
   Claire Watts

Marshall Cavendish
   Editor: Marian Armstrong
   Editorial Director: Paul Bernabeo
   Production Manager: Michael Esposito

Discovery Books
   Managing Editor: Paul Humphrey
   Project Editor: Laura Durman
   Design Concept: Ian Winton
   Designer: Barry Dwyer
   Cartographer: Stefan Chabluk
   Picture Researcher: Rachel Tisdale

The publishers would like to thank the following for their
permission to reproduce photographs:
   akg-images (Erich Lessing: 316; Ullsteinbild: 307); Art
   Directors & Trip (Ask Images: 328; Tibor Bognar: 293, 333;
   Maureen Lines: 329; Resource Foto: 305; Trip: 314, 326, 341;
   Nick and Janet Wiseman: 311); CORBIS (Bettmann: 321;
   Jonathan Blair: 339; Ed Kashi: 334; Jahangir Khan/Reuters:
   324; Mian Khursheedi/Reuters: 331; Roger Wood: 315);
   Getty Images (AFP: 342; Arif Ali/AFP: 338, 342;
   W. Harris/Hulton Archive: 319; Mohammed Mahjoub/
   AFP: 301, 302; Martin Puddy/Asia Images: 318; Robert
   Harding World Imagery: 327; Jewel Samad/AFP: 340;
   STR/AFP: 295; Keren Su/The Image Bank: 312; Time Life
   Pictures/Mansell: 317; William Vandivert/Time Life
   Pictures: 320); Christine Osborne www.copix.co.uk: 291,
   303, 308, 309, 325, 335, 337; Panos (Jeremy Horner: 292);
   Still Pictures (Sebastian Bolesch: 322; Julio Etchart: 336;
   Andreas Riedmiller: 297, 298, 300, 306, 310; Friedrich
   Stark: cover, 323; Jochen Tack: 294); World Religions Photo
   Library: 304, 332

(cover) A girl wears a bright head scarf (dupiatta) in Pakistan.

Editor's note: Many systems of dating have been used by different cultures throughout history. *Peoples of Western Asia* uses B.C.E. (Before Common Era) and C.E. (Common Era) instead of B.C. (Before Christ) and A.D. (Anno Domini, "In the Year of the Lord").

Library of Congress Cataloging-in-Publication Data

Peoples of Western Asia.
      p. cm.
   Includes bibliographical references and index.
   Contents: v. 1. Afghanistan-Armenia -- v. 2. Azerbaijan-Georgia -- v. 3. Iran-Iraq -- v. 4.
Israel-Kazakhstan -- v. 5. Kuwait-Lebanon -- v. 6. Maldives-Pakistan -- v. 7.
Qatar-Russian Federation -- v. 8. Saudi Arabia-Tajikistan -- v. 9. Turkey-Turkmenistan --
v. 10. United Arab Emirates-Yemen -- v. 11. Index.
   ISBN-13: 978-0-7614-7677-1 (set : alk. paper)
   ISBN-10: 0-7614-7677-6 (set : alk. paper)
   1. Ethnology--Asia--Encyclopedias. 2. Ethnology--MiddleEast--Encyclopedias. 3.
Asia--Encyclopedias. 4. Middle East--Encyclopedias.

DS13.P46 2006
950--dc22
                                                                        2005058213

   ISBN-13: 978-0-7614-7677-1 (set : alk. paper)
   ISBN-10: 0-7614-7677-6 (set : alk. paper)
   ISBN-13: 978-0-7614-7684-9 (v. 6 : alk. paper)
   ISBN-10: 0-7614-7684-9 (v. 6 : alk. paper)

Printed in Malaysia
11 10 09 08 07 06   6 5 4 3 2 1

Contents

Maldives   290–295
   History   290
   The Maldivians   292
   Language   292
   Religions and Beliefs   293
   The Maldives Lifestyle   293
   Economy   294
   Food and Drink   294
   Health   294
   Education in the Maldives   295
   Arts, Entertainment, and Sport   295

Oman   296–311
   Early History   297
   Arabs and Persians   298
   Islam and Imams   298
   Trade in Oman   299
   Sultans and Imams   299
   The Omani People   302
   Language   303
   Religions   304
   Festivals and Holidays   305
   Lifestyle   305
   Muslim Traditions   306
   Oman's Economy   307
   Food   308
   Health Care   309
   Education   310
   Arts, Culture, and Entertainment   310

Pakistan   312–343
   An Ancient Civilization   313
   Cities of the Indus   313
   The Aryan Culture   314
   Empires and Invaders   315
   The Coming of Islam   316
   The Mughal Empire   317
   The British Empire   318
   Independence and Partition   320
   Troubled Times   320
   Pakistan Today   322
   Pakistan's Ethnic Groups   323
   Urdu and the Mohajir   323
   In Sind   324
   Peoples of the Punjab   325
   Baluchistan   327
   Heading North   328
   An Islamic Republic   331
   Other Religions   332
   Making a Living   333
   Transportation and Communication   334
   Country and Town Life   335
   Pakistani Dishes   336
   Society and Welfare   338
   Poetry and Music   339
   Arts and Crafts   341
   Bat and Ball   342
   Festivals   343

Glossary   344

Further Reading   346

Index   347

MALDIVES

THE MALDIVES ARE AN ARCHIPELAGO OF TWENTY-SIX CORAL ATOLLS (clusters of islands) in the Indian Ocean. The archipelago covers 35,200 square miles (90,000 square kilometers) and contains 1,190 islands. Almost 80 percent of the land is less than 3 feet (1 meter) above sea level.

Most of the islands are surrounded by coral reefs, and many have shallow freshwater lagoons and white sandy beaches. Around two hundred islands are permanently inhabited, and another eighty have been developed as tourist resorts. Rising sea levels, caused by global warming, threaten the future of most Maldives islands, and the coral reefs are threatened by bleaching, another result of climate change.

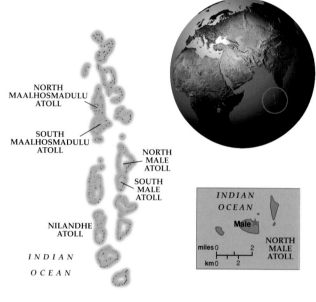

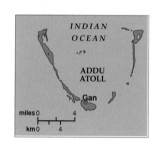

CLIMATE

The Maldives have a hot, tropical climate, and each year there are two monsoons. From November to March, the northeast monsoon brings fairly dry weather, but the southwest monsoon (from June to August) brings heavy rain. Temperatures remain very warm year round, and peak during the months of April and May.

	Male
Average January temperature:	*82°F (28°C)*
Average July temperature:	*83°F (28°C)*
Average annual precipitation:	*77 in. (196 cm)*

History

The Maldives (mahl-DEEVZ) islands are close to ancient long-distance sailing routes across the Indian Ocean. The first known migrants to settle there arrived from southern India and Sri Lanka, probably around 500 B.C.E. By around 200 C.E. the Maldives were visited by traders from

Arabia, who purchased the brightly colored shells of a sea creature called a cowrie. The shells were used as currency throughout parts of Asia and Africa, and so the Maldives became known as "the money isles." In 1153 the islands' king was converted to Islam by a traveler from northern Africa called Abu Al Barakat, who later became the Maldives' first sultan (Muslim prince).

The sultans' powers were challenged by several foreign invaders. In 1558 the Portuguese captain Andreas Andre seized

The harbor at Male, capital of the Maldives. Like most Maldivian settlements, the city is built on a low coral atoll and will be flooded if sea levels rise.

control, but he was overthrown ten years later by warrior chief Muhammad Thakurufaan. In the early seventeenth century Dutch colonists took over the islands' trade. They were replaced in the 1860s by Indian merchants. This led Muhammad Muinuddheen II, the sultan at the time, to seek help from Britain in 1867. The Maldives officially became a British

FACTS AND FIGURES

Official name: *Republic of Maldives*

Status: *Independent state*

Capital: *Male*

Major town: *Gan*

Area (land): *115 square miles (298 square kilometers)*

Population: *359,000*

Population density: *3,122 per square mile (1,205 per square kilometer)*

Peoples: *Of mixed Dravidian (from southern India), Sinhalese, and Arab descent; also Africans, Indians, and Sri Lankans*

Official language: *Maldivian Dhivehi*

Currency: *Rufiyaa*

National day: *Independence Day (July 26)*

Country's name: *The name* Maldives *comes from the Sanskrit word* Maldivipa, *which means "garland of islands."*

protectorate twenty years later, linked to Britain's colony of Ceylon (seh-LAWN: now Sri Lanka), and Britain set up a large naval base on the Addu (AH-doo) Atoll.

In 1932 the Maldives government drew up its first written constitution, which meant that the position of sultan would be elected rather than hereditary. A republic was declared in 1953 by Maldives opposition leader Amin Didi, who became president. However, the sultan was restored to office later that year. In 1957 the sultan's government, led by Prime Minister Ibrahim Nasir, became involved in a dispute with the inhabitants of the Addu and Huvadhu (hoo-VAH-doo) Atolls. The inhabitants disapproved of plans to close the British base (which employed thousands of islanders) and declared independence from the other atolls. In 1962 Nasir sent gunboats to crush the rebellion.

Time line:	First settlers arrive from India and Sri Lanka	Arab traders and Ravahe (African workers) arrive	Portuguese invasion	Dutch control Maldives' trade	The Maldives officially become a British protectorate
	ca. 500 B.C.E.	200–800 C.E.	1558	1600s–1800s	1887

Maldivian families who survived the tsunami of December 26, 2004, return to their homes one week later to inspect the damage to their houses, workshops, and farms.

off Indonesia, and many Maldives villages and tourist resorts suffered serious damage. In the Maldives, it is estimated that more than eighty people died.

The Maldivians

Maldivians (mahl-DEE-vee-uhnz), the people of the Maldives, are descended from four separate groups of settlers: Dravidians (druh-VIH-dee-yuhnz) from Kerala (keh-RAH-luh) in southern India, Dhivehi (dih-VAE-hee) from Sri Lanka, Arab traders, and African workers known as Ravahe (ruh-VAH-hee). Today these peoples no longer exist as separate communities, and most Maldivian families have ancestors from more than one ethnic group.

After 1860 Indian traders arrived to live and work in the Maldives. In the late twentieth century they were joined by workers from Sri Lanka, who found employment in the fast-growing tourist industry. These Indian and Sri Lankan communities have maintained their separate identities.

Language

The official Maldives language is Dhivehi. This developed from ancient Sinhalese, mingled with Arabic and Hindi words. It is written in Thanaa (thuh-NAH), a traditional

After a referendum in which the islanders voted to end British rule, the Maldives became an independent nation in 1968. The sultan's powers were abolished and Ibrahim Nasir was elected president. In 1978 he was replaced by Maumoon Abdul Gayoom, who remains president of the Maldives today.

At first President Gayoom won praise for his efforts to develop the Maldives economy. However, in recent years, he has been strongly criticized for his antidemocratic government and human-rights abuses. In 2004 government troops attacked hundreds of peaceful protesters and imprisoned them without trial. These events led the European Community to suspend millions of dollars worth of promised aid. In response, President Gayoom once again promised reform.

In December 2004 disaster struck in the form of a tsunami caused by an earthquake

First constitution; end of sultan's hereditary power	Rebellion by Amin Didi	Southern atoll rebellion crushed	Maldives become independent from Britain	Maumoon Abdul Gayoom elected president	Maldives hit by tsunami	President Gayoom promises reforms
1932	**1953**	**1962**	**1968**	**1978**	**2004**	**2005**

script based on Arabic that contains twenty-four letters and is written from right to left across the page. There are different local dialects in northern and southern islands, but each can be understood by "outsiders." Many Maldivians also speak English, especially in tourist resorts.

Religions and Beliefs

Being a Muslim is a legal requirement for citizenship in the Maldives, and almost all Maldivians belong to the Sunni branch of Islam. The only religious minorities are Indian merchants, who are mostly Shia Muslims, and small numbers of immigrant workers from Sri Lanka, many of whom are Buddhists. However, in the Maldives Islam is often blended with an ancient belief in jinns (JIHNZ: evil spirits), known as *fandita* (fahn-DEE-tuh). Men and women say prayers and make offerings to these spirits, or recite charms and magic spells to protect themselves and their families from harm.

Islam plays an important part in society, and the national code of law, *sariatu* (suh-ree-AH-too), is based on sharia (SHAH-ree-yuh: Muslim holy law). On most islands work stops every Friday so that men may attend communal prayers in their local *miski* (MIHSH-kee: mosque).

Most festivals and public holidays in the Maldives are based on the Islamic lunar calendar. *Kuda Id* (koo-DAH EED: the sighting of the new moon at the end of the holy month of Ramadan) is an important festival, along with the Birthday of the Prophet Muhammad. Festivals are celebrated with feasting, processions, and family parties.

Its gold dome gleaming in the hot Maldivian sun, the tall minaret (tower) of the Great Friday Mosque in Male rises from the busy street below.

The Maldives Lifestyle

Most Maldivian families are large, with at least five children. Men claim respect as the head of each family, but women are free to work outside the home, run businesses, and own goods and property. They do not take their husband's name upon marriage and are free to divorce and remarry if they wish. For many years the Maldives have had some of the highest divorce and remarriage rates in the world. However, women do keep themselves apart from men who are not close family members, especially in public places. They also dress modestly, although they do not veil their faces or cover their hair with shawls or scarves.

Around 25 percent of the population lives in Male (MAH-lae), which is home to the Maldivian government and administration, big businesses, law courts, and international aid organizations, as well as the best stores, roads, schools, and the largest hospital in the Maldives. People

living in the capital city tend to be better educated and wealthier than those living on the remote islands. Male has many narrow streets lined with both traditional-style, single-story houses and modern low-rise concrete apartment buildings. Most are made from rough stone, concrete blocks, wood, and corrugated iron.

Economy

Today the Maldives economy is based on tourism, which generates almost 60 percent of the islanders' earned income. Maldivians work at airports, on ferryboats, or for road transportation companies, as well as in hotels, restaurants, and resorts. New manufacturing plants (mostly making clothing) provide significant employment opportunities, as do more traditional industries such as boatbuilding, making handicrafts, and fishing. Smaller-scale businesses include fish and coconut processing, mining coral and sand for use in construction projects, and the weaving of mats and ropes. The taxes on all of these activities provide the government with income, together with taxes on imported goods such as food and petroleum-based fuels.

Comfortable guest villas stand on stilts in the cool, blue water at a Maldivian tourist resort. Visitors—and room service—arrive by rowing boat.

Food and Drink

Traditionally the Maldivians survived by fishing, harvesting coconuts, and growing sweet potatoes, yams, taro (TAH-roe: an edible root), millet, and watermelon. Today, however, the old ways of farming cannot produce enough to feed all the islanders and tourists, so a lot of food is imported.

Favorite dishes are based on seafood and include fried fish, curried fish, and fish soup, all accompanied by imported rice. Meat (usually beef, as Muslims do not eat pork) and chicken are served on special occasions and are often cooked with coconut and spices. Fresh fruits and ices are popular desserts, and many islanders end their meals by chewing spicy areca (uh-REE-kuh) nuts wrapped in betel (BEE-tuhl) leaves (both from the betel palm tree) and flavored with cloves and lime.

As alcohol is banned under Islam, many islanders drink only tea, coffee, fruit juices, or soda, although some enjoy *raa* (RAH), a sweet alcoholic drink made from the sap of coconut palm trees.

Health

The small size of many of the Maldives' islands, and the vast distances between them, makes the provision of health care difficult and expensive. There is also a

shortage of trained medical staff. In the 1990s international aid agencies worked with the Maldives government to set up a community health center on each of the twenty-six atolls. However, these only have the facilities to treat minor illnesses. Patients suffering from serious disease have to travel long distances to one of the Maldives' few hospitals.

Many Maldivians do not have access to a doctor, dentist, nurse, or hospital, and lack clean, safe water supplies. As a result, waterborne diseases such as typhoid and cholera are common. Malaria, tuberculosis, and leprosy are also health dangers. About six babies out of every thousand die before their first birthday, but many more children die from accidents or infections before they reach the age of five. On average, a Maldivian man can expect to live until he is around 62 years old, and a woman until she is 65.

Education in the Maldives

Maldivians value education, and almost all adults can read and write. Basic schooling is provided free of charge by the government for children 5 to 15 years old. However, some parents choose to send their children to traditional mosque schools, for which they have to pay fees. Mosque schools teach the Muslim faith, as well as reading, writing, and the Arabic language. There are no universities on the Maldives, so students wanting to study at an advanced level have to leave the islands. However, there are colleges teaching technical skills, such as construction and motor engineering.

Arts, Entertainment, and Sports

Selling traditional handicrafts has become part of the tourist industry in the Maldives. South Maalhosmadulu (mah-loes-MAH-doo-loo) Atoll (also known as the Baa Atoll) is famous for craft products, especially glossy lacquerwork and finely woven cotton sarongs. Southern Nilandhe (nih-LAND-uh) Atoll has been famous for centuries for carvings on coral stone.

Traditional music is played throughout the islands and features the pounding beat of a big *bodu beru* (BOE-doo BAE-roo: drum). It is often accompanied by energetic dancing and clapping. Thanks to modern communications, Maldives people also listen to popular music from all around the world and are able to see the latest movies.

Many Maldivians enjoy one of the world's most popular games, soccer. Water sports are very popular with tourists, especially diving, sailing, waterskiing, and surfing. Some tourists also go big-game fishing for species such as shark, but government policy decrees that all catches have to be returned to the water alive.

Dressed in clean, white uniforms, these young girls wait in a tree-shaded courtyard for classes to begin at the start of a new school year.

OMAN

THE SULTANATE OF OMAN OCCUPIES THE SOUTHEAST CORNER OF THE ARABIAN PENINSULA. It is bordered on the southwest by Saudi Arabia and Yemen and on the northwest by the United Arab Emirates.

Oman has many offshore islands, including Maşīrah and the Jazā'ir Khurīyā Murīyā group. Oman's territory also includes the northern tip of the Musandam Peninsula, together with several small islands nearby.

This is a very important area as it gives Oman control of the Strait of Hormuz—a seaway used by all ships entering or leaving the Persian Gulf.

The landscape of Oman is dramatic and varied. Most of the country is a high, stony, desert plateau. In the west, this forms part of the harsh and forbidding Rub' al-Khali Desert, where few living creatures can survive. To the east, the Wahiba Sands consists of constantly shifting sand dunes.

Rugged mountain ranges run along the north and south of the country. Oman's highest peak, Mount Al-Akhdar, at 10,086 feet (3,074 meters), towers over the Al-Hajar range in the north. Spectacular wadis (steep narrow valleys, with hidden caves and water holes) cut through the lower slopes. There is also a narrow strip of fine, white sandy beaches around the coast.

CLIMATE

Oman has an arid, subtropical climate. From April to October inland areas are very dry and extremely hot. Coastal regions are slightly cooler, and from June to September monsoon winds from the Arabian Sea bring mist and drizzle to the Al-Qarā Mountains and the southern coast. From November to March, the weather throughout Oman is hot, with occasional heavy rainfall.

	Masqat	Thamarīt
Average January temperature:	71°F (22°C)	66°F (19°C)
Average July temperature:	94°F (34°C)	87°F (31°C)
Average annual precipitation:	4 in. (10 cm)	2.5 in. (6 cm)

Africa, spices from India, and pearls from the Arabian coast.

After around 500 B.C.E. Oman's wealth was derived from its control of the world trade in frankincense and myrrh (resin from trees). Omani merchants made long journeys by land and by sea to Persia (PER-zhuh: now Iran), India, and lands around the Mediterranean Sea (including Egypt, Greece, and the Roman Empire).

Like children all around the world, these young Omani boys enjoy playing and laughing together. For most Omani families, having children is a source of pride and delight.

Early History

The earliest traces of human habitation in Oman (oe-MAHN) are stone tombs in the north of the country, dating from around 3500 B.C.E. The people who built them probably lived by growing dates, wheat and barley, and catching fish along the coast. These early farmers traded with travelers from the Indus (IHN-doos) Valley region and Baluchistan (buh-LOO-kih-stan: now part of Pakistan and Afghanistan). They may also have built boats.

By around 2500 B.C.E. the wealthy Mangan (MANG-gan) Empire ruled northern Oman. Its riches came from mining copper and selling it to Elam (eh-LAHM: now southern Iran) and Sumer (SOO-muhr: now southern Iraq), where it was used to make weapons. Traders from Mangan also sold timber from eastern

FACTS AND FIGURES

Official name: *Sultanate of Oman*

Status: *Independent state*

Capital: *Masqat*

Major towns: *Maṭraḥ, Salālah, Sūr, Nizwā*

Area: *82,000 square miles (212,380 square kilometers)*

Population: *3,100,000*

Population density: *38 per square mile (15 per square kilometer)*

Peoples: *73 percent Arab; 27 percent other (including Baluchi, Indian, Pakistani, Sri Lankan, Bangladeshi, and African resident workers, plus European, North American, and Australian expatriates)*

Official language: *Arabic*

Currency: *Omani rial*

National day: *Birthday of Sultan Qaboos (November 18)*

Country's name: *The word* Oman *either came from an Arabic word meaning "settled" or from the name of an early Arab leader.*

Time line:	First traces of human habitation in Oman	Persians control northern Oman; settlers arrive from Greece	Arab tribes migrate to Oman	Arab tribes drive Persians out of Oman
	ca. 3500 B.C.E	ca. 560 B.C.E.	ca. 200–700 C.E.	ca. 600

In the past, the resin from spiky frankincense trees was more valuable than gold. Today it is still gathered slowly and carefully by hand.

Luban (Frankincense)

Oman is one of the few countries in the world in which frankincense trees can grow. They belong to a genus (group) of trees called **Boswellia.** *Frankincense resin, or* luban *(LOO-bahn), as it is called in Oman, is obtained by making small cuts in the tree trunks. The sap that oozes out is collected and then left to dry and solidify. Little chunks of solid sap can either be burned to give off a sweet-smelling smoke or dissolved in oil and mixed with other substances to create perfumes. The Omani people use frankincense to freshen their homes and their clothes.*

Arabs and Persians

Oman's wealth attracted both traders and invaders. From around 560 B.C.E. northern Oman was controlled by Persians (PERZH-yuhnz), who built trading ports around the coast. Colonists also migrated from Greece. Around 200 C.E. new groups of Arab settlers began to arrive, mostly from Yemen. At first Arabs and Persians lived fairly peacefully together. Arab tribes continued their traditional rural lifestyle, growing crops, raising livestock, or traveling as nomads in the desert, while many of the Persians were townspeople and traders. However, as the Arab population increased, Arab tribes took over more land, and by around 600 they had driven the Persians out of Oman.

Islam and Imams

During the seventh century, Arabs from the cities of Medina (meh-DEE-nuh) and Mecca (MEHK-uh) in Saudi Arabia spread a new faith called Islam throughout the Arabian Peninsula. From around 660 Oman was ruled by the powerful Muslim Umayyad (OO-mie-yahd) dynasty, based in Damascus (duh-MAHS-kuhs), in Syria. Between 746 and 748, however, an Omani general, Talib al-Haqq, led an army of tribesmen against the Umayyads, and the Umayyads lost control of Oman.

The Omani rebellion was inspired by religion and a wish for political freedom.

Oman ruled by Umayyad dynasty	General Talib al-Haqq leads rebellion against Umayyad rule	First Ibadi imam is elected	Oman invaded by many different Middle Eastern peoples	Portuguese explorer Vasco da Gama arrives in Oman
ca. 660	**746–748**	**749**	**ca. 750–1500**	**1498**

The Arab tribes who lived in Oman honored a radical Muslim preacher, Abdullah bin Ibad. He taught that Muslims should live in communities ruled by imams (spiritual and political leaders), who would teach them how to lead good lives. Each imam should be chosen by the community, and could be removed from power if he failed to uphold Muslim religious law. Ibad's followers became known as Ibadis. Other Muslims said that their beliefs were wrong and possibly dangerous.

In 749 the Omani people elected their first imam. Ibadi imams led the tribes in Oman for the next seven hundred years, but they faced frequent attacks from hostile Muslim rulers. From 1154 onward, northern and eastern Oman was controlled by Muslim kings from Hormuz (hoe-MOOZ), in Persia. Oman was also attacked by Persians, Turks, and Mongols, who hoped to share in the country's wealth.

Trade in Oman

Throughout these upheavals Omani trade continued to prosper. Its largest city, Şuḥār (soo-HAHR), on the north coast, was described by a Muslim geographer around 950 as "the wealthiest city in any Muslim land." Omani merchants sailed northward to the Middle East and eastward to India. There they met traders from China and the Southeast Asian islands.

By the fifteenth century Oman's international trading contacts made it a rich prize for European explorers. In 1498 Portuguese explorer Vasco da Gama visited Oman. In 1506 the Portuguese returned

with guns, and the following year they took control of Oman. By 1515 the Portuguese were collecting taxes on all ships entering the Gulf. Omani tribes fought against Portuguese invaders; rival British and Dutch ships also attacked them. For safety, the Portuguese built new forts at the port of Masqat (MUHS-kat) and defended the city with strong walls. However, in 1650 Omanis, led by Imam Sultan bin Saif, captured Masqat and drove the Portuguese from Oman.

Over the next century strong imams conquered and occupied Portuguese settlements in eastern Africa and the Persian Gulf. Omani merchants began to deal in slaves and guns as well as incense and spices. Trading ports such as Masqat developed closer links with the rich overseas settlements, neglecting the poor, unprofitable Omani inland regions.

In 1741 armies led by Imam Ahmad bin Said defeated Persian invaders. He made Masqat his capital city and took the title of sultan (prince). He founded a new dynasty that still rules Oman today. In the early nineteenth century, his descendant Sayyid Said bin Sultan enlarged the Omani Empire by taking control of the fertile Dhofar (doe-FAHR) region. When Sultan Sayyid died in 1856, Omani lands were divided among his sons. Oman itself was ruled by his son Faisal bin Turki.

Sultans and Imams

Tribes from inland Oman challenged Sultan Faisal's right to rule. Following Ibadi tradition, they wanted a leader they had

Portuguese troops invade Oman	Portugal controls Oman and the Strait of Hormuz waterway	Portuguese driven out of Oman	Oman conquers settlements in eastern Africa and the Persian Gulf
1506	**1515**	**1650**	**ca. 1650–1750**

This magnificent fort towers 165 feet (50 meters) above the town of Bahlā' in northern Oman. Parts of the building are more than fifteen hundred years old.

Forts and Watchtowers

There are around five hundred forts (small castles) and watchtowers still surviving in Oman. Most are at least three hundred years old, though many have been rebuilt over the centuries and restored or preserved in recent years. Forts were built to protect Omani trading towns, as jails, and as residences for army commanders. They had walls 7 feet (2 meters) thick and tall towers from which cannonballs were fired. Watchtowers were tall buildings, built close to paths and coasts. Troops of armed guards were stationed there and sent urgent messages warning rulers, soldiers, and citizens of approaching invaders. Some forts and watchtowers are still used by the Omani police and armed forces today.

chosen themselves, rather than someone who had inherited the title. Faisal died in 1913, and the tribes elected Imam Isa bin Saleh to rule, refusing to obey Faisal's son, Sultan Taimur. In 1915 the tribes tried to take power, but they were defeated by British troops who agreed to help the sultan because he controlled shipping routes used by British fleets. In 1920 Sultan Taimur and the rebel tribes made an uneasy peace. They agreed that an elected imam would be the religious leader of all of Oman and have political power over some inland areas.

In 1938 a new sultan, Said bin Taimur, came to power. He held strict, traditional views on government, politics, and religion, and he did not want Oman to be modernized. He cut Oman off from the rest of the world, and Omanis were not allowed to travel, even within their own country. Only a few trusted families could take part in foreign trade. Radios and most books were banned, as was the wearing of glasses, and education was strongly discouraged.

Sultan Said tried to control the inland tribes and in 1954 accused the imam of siding with his enemies. The following year his army occupied land where the imam's strongest supporters lived. Again the sultan was helped by Britain, who now hoped to find oil in Oman. Fighting continued until

Imam Ahmad bin Said defeats Persian invaders and founds new ruling dynasty	Omani Empire divided; Faisal bin Turki rules Oman	Sultan Taimur recognizes imam as spiritual leader of Oman	Sultan Said bin Taimur rules Oman	Rebellion by Omani tribes
1741	**1856**	**1920**	**1938–1970**	**1955–1959**

1959, when the imam was deported. In 1965 rebellions began in the far south of the country. They were led by the Dhofar Liberation Front and helped by China and South Yemen, who hoped to introduce communist rule. In the same year, the United Nations called for an end to British influence in Oman.

Oil was discovered in Oman in 1964 and exports began in 1967, but Sultan Said refused to spend oil revenues to develop his country. In 1970 he was peacefully removed from power by his only son, Qaboos bin Said, who still rules as sultan of Oman today. In 1973 Sultan Qaboos asked Britain and Iran for help to crush the Dhofar rebellion. Although fighting ended in 1975, peace was not agreed until 1982.

Sultan Qaboos abolished most of his father's strict laws. He allowed Omani people to travel, trade, and make contact with the outside world, although even today use of the Internet is controlled, and so is the press. Sultan Qaboos also launched a series of five-year plans to use oil revenues to modernize and develop Oman and to pay for welfare proposals. In the past thirty years these have transformed Oman from a poor, undeveloped country to a prosperous modern state.

Oman is not yet a democracy. The position of sultan is hereditary, passing from father to son. The sultan is head of state, government leader, commander of the armed forces, and in charge of foreign affairs; he also plans policies, makes new laws, and chooses government ministers. The first female government minister was appointed in 2004. The sultan is advised by two Majlis (MAHJ-lees: councils), whose task is to offer comments and make suggestions. There are no political parties, but council members are elected by the public every four years. All Omani citizens over the age of 21—including women—are entitled to vote.

The Omani legal system combines English and Muslim law. Punishments include the death penalty. Judges are independent, though appeals can be made to the sultan.

For most of his reign Sultan Qaboos has followed an independent foreign policy, encouraging contact between Oman and other nations with widely differing policies and views. Oman is also a founding member of the Gulf Cooperation Council, an association of Arabian Peninsula states. In 1991, during the Gulf War, the sultan

Omani women wait to vote at a polling station in Masqat in October 2003. For the first time all Omani citizens had the right to vote for members of the two national Majlis.

Oil discovered in Oman	Rebellion by Dhofar Liberation Front	Sultan Qaboos bin Said takes power	Oman becomes founding member of Gulf Cooperation Council	Allied forces use Omani air bases during First Gulf War
1964	**1965–1982**	**1970**	**1981**	**1991**

His Majesty Sultan Qaboos, the ruler of Oman since 1970, inspects a military parade in Masqat on his birthday, and his country's national day, November 18, 2004.

of them had been released. The Omani economy continues to develop, in line with the government's latest five-year plan. The plan aims to reduce the nation's dependence on oil exports, create jobs, build infrastructure (such as roads and hospitals), develop financial services, encourage trade and tourism, and replace overseas workers with trained Omani personnel.

The Omani People

The inhabitants of Oman are divided into two distinct groups, each with separate legal rights, lifestyles, and, often, living conditions. The majority of the population is made up of Omani citizens, but there are more than half a million nonnationals who live and work in Oman.

Most Omani citizens are descended from Arab tribes who migrated to the region during the past two thousand years. A few, such as the Wahibas (wah-HEE-buhz) from the eastern desert and the Jabalis (juh-BAH-leez) from the southern Al-Qarā (ahl-KAH-ruh) Mountains, still live in traditional tribal communities containing many related families. They trust in tribal values, such as honor, bravery, loyalty, and equality. However, because of Oman's long history as a trading nation and its position close to international sea routes, many Omani citizens have at least one ancestor from a non-Arab country or community.

Nonnationals in Oman are mostly of south Asian or east African origin. Workers from India, Pakistan, Bangladesh, Sri Lanka, and east African lands once ruled by Oman have traveled to the country in

allowed Allied forces, led by the United States and Britain, to use Omani air bases. In 1999 and 2003, he signed treaties with neighboring United Arab Emirates, ending a long-running dispute over border territory. In 2001 British forces trained in the Omani desert while preparing to attack the *Taliban* (TAH-lee-bahn) in Afghanistan as part of the international War on Terror (see AFGHANISTAN).

In contrast with several other countries in the Gulf region, Oman remains relatively peaceful, and increasingly prosperous. The government continues its antiterrorist policies, which include deporting unofficial migrant workers from countries known to shelter Islamic fundamentalists. In January 2005 nearly one hundred Omanis were arrested and imprisoned, accused of belonging to an Islamic terrorist organization. However, by June 2005 all

Oman agrees border treaties with United Arab Emirates	British forces train in Oman before attacking the Taliban in Afghanistan	Members of suspected Islamic terrorist organization arrested by Omani government and later released
1999 and 2003	**2001**	**2005**

search of employment. Unlike Omani citizens, they cannot vote or stand for election, are not entitled to government health care and education benefits, and can be told to leave the country at any time. Even so, most hope to earn higher wages and find better living conditions than they would at home, and spend most of their working lives in Oman. Many send a large portion of their earnings back to their families in their homeland.

There are also expatriates working in Oman from Palestine, Jordan, Syria, Egypt, Europe, the Philippines, Australia, and the United States. Most are employed on short-term contracts and plan to return home eventually.

In recent years the government has introduced "Omanization" polices to replace nonnational and expatriate workers with local Omani people. It believes that this is the only way to avoid unemployment, poverty, and idleness among citizens; to establish a skilled, trained local workforce; and to ensure that Oman's economy develops for the good of Omani society as a whole. Because of this, Omani citizens are often employed in low-status, poor-paying jobs, such as laboring, that are performed by nonnationals in other rich Gulf states.

Language

The official language of Oman is Arabic. There are several regional dialects; each can be difficult for strangers to understand. Devout Muslims may also study Classical

Traditional Clothes

Most Omani citizens choose to wear traditional dress. It is actually a legal requirement for those working for the government. However, it is illegal for foreigners to wear this clothing (including nonnationals). Omani men wear a long, loose robe called a dishdasha *(deesh-DAHSH-uh), which is usually white or light purple. Underneath they wear a sarong or length of cloth wrapped around the waist called a* wizar *(wih-ZEER). Their heads are covered by a* kumma *(KOO-muh: embroidered cap) or a* massar *(muh-SAHR: turban). Women can also wear a dishdasha, or choose a different type of robe called a* kandoura *(kahn-DOO-rah), worn with* sirwal *(seer-WAHL: baggy pants) underneath. Both are made of brightly colored fabric, printed with vivid floral designs, and may be trimmed with heavy gold embroidery. On formal occasions or in public places, women cover their bright clothes with a long black cloak, called an* abaya *(ah-BIE-uh). Some choose to wear a burka (BUR-kah), which covers the face with a mesh panel, but this is not compulsory.*

Omani men wear traditional dishdasha robes, kummas (embroidered caps), and turbans as they wait for trading to begin at the date market in Sanāw in northern Oman.

Arabic. This is the traditional, very poetic, version of Arabic used in the Muslim holy book, the Koran. Muslims believe that the Koran is literally the Word of God and say that Classical Arabic is "the language of the angels."

Educated Omani men and women, together with the government, most businesses, radio, television, and other media, use Modern Standard Arabic. This is a simplified, up-to-date version of Classical Arabic and is understood throughout Oman and the whole Gulf region, enabling Arabs from different places to communicate with one another. English is often spoken as a second language and is used in international businesses and in the travel and tourist industries. Nonnationals living in Oman may speak the language of their homeland.

Religions

Almost all Omani citizens follow the faith of Islam, and so do many resident nonnationals. A large majority of Omani citizens (about three-fourths of the population) belong to the Ibadi branch of Islam; others are Sunnis and Shias.

Oman is now the only place in the world where large numbers of Ibadis still live. Belief in Ibadi Islam, which is conservative, but also moderate and tolerant, is strongest

Young boys sit with their teacher at a Koran school in an Omani mosque. The floor and walls are covered with beautiful carpets as a sign of respect for Allah (God).

in country areas. Sunni Muslims make up almost one-fourth of Oman's population and live mainly in the southern Dhofar region and around Sūr (SOOR) in the northeast. In the far north, and around the capital city, Masqat, there are small communities of Shia Muslims. Many are nonnationals from Iran and Iraq.

Whatever branch of Islam they follow, religion plays an important part in the lives of Omani Muslims. Religious scholarship and knowledge of the Koran win respect and influence, at work and in government. Praying together encourages feelings of solidarity among Omani men. Most Omani conversations contain references to God. For example, friends will arrange to meet, "Inshallah" (ihn-shah-LAH: God willing), and say goodbye with the words "Allah yisullmak" (uh-LAH ihs-OOL-muhk: God protect you). Omani law is based on Muslim principles, and many social customs have their roots in Islam.

Freedom of religion is guaranteed by Omani law, although non-Muslims are not allowed to enter mosques. There are small numbers of Hindus living in Oman (mostly nonnationals from India) and some Christians (mainly expatriates from Europe and the United States).

Festivals and Holidays

The most important Omani holidays are Muslim religious festivals and the national day, Sultan Qaboos' birthday on November 18. Many people have a week's vacation around the time of the national day; all shops, factories, and offices are closed, and the streets are decorated with portraits of the sultan. Workers spend time with their families—at home, at beach resorts, in the countryside, or visiting friends. They may also watch army parades with rousing music, spectacular firework shows, and athletic displays by children wearing bright, colorful costumes.

Religious festivals include Lailat ul-Miraj (luh-EE-luht uhl-mih-RAHJ), the night when the Prophet Muhammad experienced a revelation of heaven; Eid ul-Adha (EED uhl-AHD-hah), a four-day celebration that commemorates the Prophet Abraham's obedience to God; and Eid ul-Fitr (EED uhl-FEET-ruh), the joyful feast at the end of the holy month of Ramadan, when Omanis sing, play music, and dance. During

Old and new houses—and air-conditioned, modern cars— line the corniche (scenic road) that runs along the Gulf coast in the Maṭraḥ district of Oman's capital city.

daylight hours in Ramadan, everyone in Oman (including non-Muslims) is banned from eating or drinking in public. As soon as darkness falls, however, friends welcome guests to meals in their homes, or stroll through the busy streets listening to music and enjoying beverages and snacks from market stalls that stay open all night long.

Lifestyle

Oman is a land of contrasts. Almost half the population lives in the crowded capital city of Masqat or along the nearby northeast coast. In the late twentieth century, Masqat greatly expanded in size. Two new cities, Ruwī (ROO-ee) and Maṭraḥ (MAH-truh), were built beside it, creating a huge metropolis covering 50 square miles (130 square kilometers). Masqat remains the historic capital, with the sultan's palace and many fine old merchant houses, together with massive ancient walls, gates, and impressive forts. Maṭraḥ is the port area and Ruwī is a business district. There are also sprawling residential areas, industrial districts, warehouses, shopping malls, museums and galleries, concert halls, offices, hotels, and restaurants. Outside the

city limits, there are irrigated fields where farmers grow fruit, vegetables, dates, and coconuts.

All new buildings in Oman have to follow government rules: they should be well built, with modern amenities (such as air-conditioning), but still be in keeping with Oman's traditional architectural styles. There are no skyscrapers made of glass and steel. Instead most buildings are not high, and feature materials such as stone and brick, or decorative Islamic tiles. Many houses and apartment buildings are planned around courtyards, which offer privacy and security. The most luxurious have gardens and pools. In many homes and public buildings, there are separate living and working rooms for women and men.

Dhofar, in the south, is the next most populated area. Around 200,000 people live there in towns and villages on the lower slopes of the mountains or along the coast. They collect frankincense, work in the tourist industry, or make a living as farmers. High up in the mountains, the nomadic Jofari (juh-FAH-ree) people tend herds of cattle. A further thirty thousand people live in traditional fishing villages or modern army bases on the Musandam Peninsula.

In comparison, the rest of Oman is sparsely populated. Its dry, desert landscape makes farming impossible, except at scattered oases. The Bedouin (BEHD-oo-wihn: nomad tribes) who live there follow a traditional nomadic lifestyle. They lead herds of camels and goats in search of water and fresh grass. They live in black tents woven from goat hair or in shelters called *barasti* (buh-RAHS-tee), made from palm tree fronds (leaves). From time to time they visit oasis towns to trade.

The traditional Bedouin life is very hard, and modern influences have gradually

Although this Omani woman has chosen to wear a burka (mask), she still wishes to look attractive. Her mask is made of glossy, colored silk and she wears traditional makeup.

begun to affect the ancient traditions. Many Bedouin have bought radios, cell phones, and satellite televisions and built shelters from metal mesh panels. They will sometimes spend weeks living in just one place so that their children can receive medical care and attend school. They replaced some of their camels with rugged pickup trucks. Many now carry food and water to their animals in wagons rather than roaming the desert in search of oases.

Muslim Traditions

In 1994 Sultan Qaboos remarked, "A people without a heritage also has no future." Omani people are very proud of their country's history and their traditional way of life. They wish to preserve them while also benefiting from the scientific and technological advances of the modern world. Omani traditions are based on ancient Arab tribal customs blended with the religious teachings of Islam.

Family is very important to most Omanis. All adults expect to marry and have children. They look forward to enjoying large family gatherings, such as weddings, where celebrations often continue for several days. They also expect to rely on relatives to help them with child care, in business, or in times of trouble. In return, they are happy to help family members whenever they can.

Courtesy, to both friends and strangers, is also highly valued. Omanis exchange friendly greetings when they meet, such as "Tisbah ala khair" (TIHZ-buh uh-luh KAH-eer: May the morning find you well), and men often shake hands. It is considered very bad manners to show anger or impatience, or to swear in front of other people. Instead Omani men and women aim to remain calm, dignified, and gracious in public at all times.

Generous hospitality is another valued tradition. Today most Omanis regard welcoming visitors as a pleasant duty. Even business meetings start with several minutes of greetings and cheerful conversation, together with offers of tea or coffee.

As Muslims, Omanis feel that modesty is an important part of their religion. Open displays of affection between men and women are taboo. Males and females sit separately in all public places, from mosques to taxis and buses. Many restaurants and beaches have private spaces for families, or for women and young children only; Omani women play sports and go swimming fully clothed.

Oman's Economy

Until 1964, when oil was discovered in Oman, most country people survived by fishing and farming and town dwellers made their living as traders and craft workers. Today farmers produce dates, limes, bananas, and vegetables and raise

Women's Lives

In spite of traditional customs, Omani women lead busy, active lives. By law they are free to work, drive, shop, study, or travel. Many young Omani women are well educated and wish to have careers as well as families. Some run businesses from home, often in traditional women's industries such as weaving and needlecraft. Others go out to work in a wide range of occupations, from medicine and engineering to journalism and fashion design. More than one-third of all government employees are women. They work as nurses, teachers, librarians, administrators, and accountants.

A female researcher at an Omani medical laboratory peers down a microscope. Women now hold positions in many skilled professions in Oman.

camels and cattle for sale. However, oil production, together with natural gas extraction and copper mining (both developed in the 1980s), has transformed the Omani economy during the past thirty years. Major industries include copper smelting, chemical manufacturing, construction, banking, food processing, and service industries such as catering, tourism, media, and transportation.

Oman's natural resources of oil and gas are substantial, but not as large as those in other, nearby Gulf states. For this reason the Omani government has encouraged the development of industries that do not rely on oil in an effort to ensure employment and prosperity when the national oil and gas reserves run out. Omani citizens train in business management, metallurgy (the science of metals), and information technology. Oman's ports have been developed as major transshipment areas for long-distance international trade. The government has invited overseas companies to invest in Oman and has developed new high-tech enterprises, such as the manufacture of fiber optics.

Food

Traditionally Omani food was based on local products—dates, fresh and dried fish, and milk and meat from camels. For special occasions, rice and spices, especially cloves, cardamom, turmeric, and saffron, were added. Today Oman's shops, market stalls, and restaurants sell many different foods from all over the world.

Even so, Omanis often choose to eat traditional foods from the Gulf region. These include flat *rukhal* (roo-KAHL) bread, which is made without yeast; yogurt; pilaf (PEE-lahf: spiced rice with little pieces of meat); *moutabel* (MOO-tuh-behl: eggplant and sesame seed dip); *makhbousa* (muhk-BOO-suh: rice and meat stew seasoned with dried limes); *qabooli* (kuh-BOOL-lee: spiced rice); *maqudeed* (MAH-koo-deed: strips of dried meat); and *shuwa* (SHOO-wuh: spiced roast lamb, goat, or camel, cooked slowly in a clay oven). All meat sold in Oman must be halal (huh-LAHL: from animals that

Seated on the floor in traditional style, three generations of an Omani family share a simple meal of halvah (sweet sesame seed candy), dates, and oranges, together with coffee.

Dates and Honey

Omani people are famous for their love of sweet food. More than eighty different types of date palms grow in Oman, and their sweet, sticky fruits are made into syrup, served as snacks, and used as ingredients in many dishes, including savory meat stews. Honey is also very popular and was traditionally collected from the hives of wild bees in tree trunks in the Al-Hajar Mountains. In the late twentieth century modern methods of beekeeping were introduced to Oman, and honey production has greatly increased.

have been slaughtered according to Muslim religious laws). Like other Muslims, Omani people do not eat pork.

Many meals are served with fresh crisp lettuce and tomatoes, or with baked vegetables. Tomatoes, sweet peppers, eggplants, and zucchini may also be stuffed with meat, rice, and spices. Omani meals do not usually include dessert, but dates, sweet pastries, nuts, and fresh fruit are eaten as snacks. The favorite Omani candy is halvah (HAHL-vuh), a sticky mixture of sesame seed pulp, honey, and nuts.

Candy and snacks are usually served with tiny cups of *qahwa* (kuh-WAH: Arabic coffee). Typically this is unsweetened, and may be flavored with cardamom. Some people prefer Arab-style tea, served very sweet and with mint leaves floating on top. Other traditional Omani beverages include camel's milk, *laban* (luh-BAHN: buttermilk), and *zatar* (zuh-TAHR: herb tea). Fruit juices, soda, bottled spring water, and milk

A trained nurse cares for her patient in a modern Omani hospital. Oman's medical facilities have been transformed since 1970 and are now among the best in the world.

flavored with ginger or rose water are also popular. Omani Muslims do not consume alcohol, and the sale of alcoholic beverages is strictly controlled by the government.

Health Care

In 1970 Oman had just one hospital, run by missionaries from the United States, and a few small government health centers. Standards of public hygiene were poor. When Sultan Qaboos came to power, improving health care and hygiene was one of his top priorities. Today Oman has some of the most up-to-date hospitals in the world, run by well-trained professionals. However, these are mostly sited in cities and towns, and access to a doctor can still be difficult in remote regions. To solve this problem, the government is encouraging health workers to move to the country.

Health care is provided free by the government for all citizens of Oman. Emergency treatment is free to nonnationals, but they have to pay for other medical and dental care. Streets, shops, and public

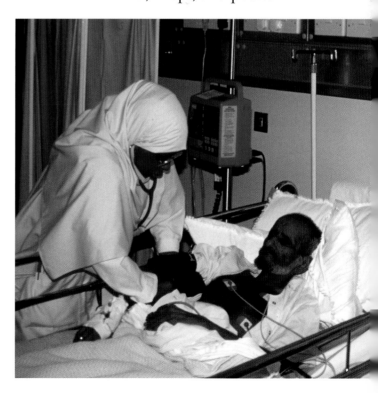

buildings are now much cleaner, and safe drinking water has been provided to most homes. Mass immunization campaigns have protected children against serious infections, such as polio, although there are still cases of malaria and tuberculosis. As a result of all these changes, a baby boy born today can expect to live until he is 71 years old; a baby girl until she is 75.

Khanjars (Daggers)

Traditionally all Omani men carried a khanjar *(KHAN-jahr: sharp, hook-shaped dagger), which hung from a belt around the waist. It was used in war as a weapon and in peacetime as a knife. The blade was made of steel, and the scabbard (cover) was richly decorated all over with patterns made from thin sheets of silver or hammered silver wire. The handle was made of rhino horn, imported from eastern Africa. Today khanjars are mainly worn on special occasions (some tribespeople still carry them every day). Modern khanjars have sharp, steel blades and decorated scabbards, but their handles are mostly made of plastic or wood.*

Education

The Omani government—and Omani families—believe that education is very important, but until Sultan Qaboos came to power in 1970, only Omani boys could go to school. Today almost 50 percent of school and college students are female, and there are many female teachers and professors.

The state provides free education for all children of Omani citizens between the ages of 6 and 17. In the past thirty years the government has built more than one thousand new schools, and thousands of Omanis have trained to be teachers. Classes in state schools are taught in Arabic, with English as a second language. There are separate classrooms and sports areas for girls and boys. After leaving school, students can continue their education at state-run colleges, or at Sultan Qaboos University. The government plans to build more universities very soon.

There are more than one hundred private schools in Oman. Some cater to children from wealthy Omani families; others teach the children of expatriates and nonnationals. Standards in all Omani schools are usually high, although the rapid development of the education system has occasionally led to problems, such as a lack of resources and large class sizes in some areas.

The Omani government also runs adult education programs to teach basic literacy and technical subjects to citizens who did not have the chance to go to school when they were young.

Arts, Culture, and Entertainment

Omani craftspeople are famous for their metalworking skills. Bedouin silversmiths (all men) make large, impressive jewelry, hammered and stamped with intricate patterns and designs. Traditionally jewelry was a way of storing and transporting wealth, and a bride was given as much as her family could afford on her wedding day. Omani men carried khanjars with decorated silver handles, silver gunpowder holders, and silver boxes containing kohl (a sticky black paste, worn like eyeliner and believed to protect the eyes from disease).

Weaving was traditionally an Omani woman's task. Weavers made rugs, blankets, bags, and cushion covers from goat and camel hair, colored with natural plant dyes. They also wove the fronds (leaves) of date palm into all kinds of useful items, such as mats, baskets, and fans. Today these traditional skills still exist in country areas, but most Omani women buy household items and textiles from shops.

There are a few movie theaters in big Omani cities, and most families have a television and a radio, which plays the latest Arabic pop songs. Many Omani people still enjoy traditional entertainments, especially music, singing, and dancing. Omani music blends Arabic styles and those of eastern Africa, and is played on the

Falconry and Bull Butting

In the past, hunting with falcons was a way of finding food in Oman. Trained falcons caught houbara *(hoo-BAH-ruh: birds somewhat like chickens) that lived in the desert. Today falconry is a favorite Omani sport. Falcons are bred in captivity and specially trained before being sold for high prices. Their owners—who often live in cities—take them to the countryside to hunt birds and small mammals during their leisure time.*

Bull butting is another traditional sport that continues today. Pairs of bulls fight each other by butting violently with their heads. Although the butting looks and sounds violent, the bulls are not killed in the fighting and are rarely injured. Around twenty bulls take part in each contest, and many Omani towns have a bullring.

tamboura (tahm-BOO-rah: harp), *oud* (OOD: lute), drums, tambourines, huge seashells (blown like trumpets), wild deer horns, and goatskin bagpipes. Musicians often accompany lively groups of dancers, and favorite dances include the *liwa* (LEE-wah: to a fast African rhythm), the *ayyalah* (ie-YAH-luh: a Bedouin dance celebrating courage), and the *na'ashat* (nah-SHAHT: danced only by young girls).

Seated in front of the Al Sanwa clock tower (a famous local landmark on the edge of Masqat), Omani musicians perform on oud (lute), drum, and tambourine.

PAKISTAN

PAKISTAN FORMS A BRIDGE BETWEEN CENTRAL ASIA AND THE INDIAN SUBCONTINENT. It includes some of the world's most spectacular mountain summits, as well as plateaus, deserts, and plains, crossed by rivers that drain into the Arabian Sea. Pakistan also has large, busy cities and is the world's seventh most populated country. It is bordered to the west by Iran and Afghanistan, to the northeast by China, and by India to the east.

Low mountains and hills form barriers in the northwest and west of the country. Northern highlands rise to the dazzling snows of the Hindu Kush and Karakoram Mountains, where the peak of Tirich Mir reaches 25,260 feet (7,700 meters) above sea level.

Five rivers are fed by the northern mountains: the Jhelum, Chenab, Ravi, Sutlej, and Beas (in India). These give their name to the Punjab ("five waters") region of central Pakistan and northwest India. All flow into the great Indus River, which forms a delta on the Arabian Sea. The irrigated southern plains are hemmed in by the Thar Desert in the southeast and the arid plateau of Baluchistan in the southwest.

A young girl returns from the fields to the town of Karimabad, in the mountainous Hunza region. Pakistan's far north has been opened up by the building of the Karakoram Highway to China.

312

An Ancient Civilization

The Indus (IHN-doos) Valley was a center of agriculture from at least 3500 B.C.E. Its broad plains were enriched with mud deposited by annual floods. The ancient course and flow of the river was different from that of today, and the region as a whole was wetter and more fertile.

Cities of the Indus

During the following millennium, the first large towns on the Indian subcontinent were built in the Indus Valley. Between 2500 and 2000 B.C.E. the various communities developed a unified culture,

CLIMATE

Most of Pakistan enjoys three seasons. The coolest period lasts from October to February. Temperatures then increase until July, when monsoon winds bring rain to many southern and central regions. Northern Pakistan is affected by the continental climate of central Asia, with its extremes of heat and cold. Arid conditions prevail in the southeast, southwest, and parts of the north. Temperatures in the southern Sind region can climb to 122°F (50°C), while at high altitudes in the north they can drop to −2°F (−19°C).

	Islamabad	Karachi
Average January temperature:	51°F (11°C)	66°F (19°C)
Average July temperature:	85°F (29°C)	86°F (30°C)
Average annual precipitation:	43 in. (109 cm)	9 in. (23 cm)

one of the world's great early civilizations. It is not known for sure how the cities were governed, but many archaeologists have come to the conclusion that they were ruled by priest-kings. There was a common script used by the Indus peoples, which has yet to be fully deciphered.

The surrounding countryside produced wheat, barley, vegetables, and cotton.

Time line:	Agriculture in the Indus Valley	Rise of Indus Valley civilization	Settlements at Harappa and Mohenjo Daro
	3500 B.C.E.	2500–2000 B.C.E.	ca. 2000 B.C.E.

Harappa and Mohenjo Daro

Perhaps as many as a hundred major settlements thrived on the Indus plains, the largest of which were at Harappa (huh-RAH-puh), in the Punjab (PUHN-jahb), and Mohenjo Daro (moe-HAEN-joe DAH-roe), in Sind (SIHND). More than two thousand years ago these two walled cities each had a total area of around 150 acres (60 hectares), with a planned grid of broad streets and populations of around forty thousand. Houses were built of baked bricks, manufactured to a standard size. Large houses had two stories, with courtyards and flat roofs, and smaller houses comprised a single room. There were bathrooms and streets with drains. In the middle of each city was a raised area or citadel, which served as a center for religious ceremonies, such as ritual bathing, as well as government administration.

This bearded figure wearing a decorative shawl dates from around 2100 B.C.E. It comes from the lower town at Mohenjo Daro and may represent a priest-king or perhaps a god.

There were public granaries for the storage of food and supplies. Cattle provided meat and milk, while their dung was used as fuel for cooking. Oxen were used for pulling carts and plowing, and sheep, hogs, and dogs were also raised.

Around the edges of the Indus cities were craft workshops that produced pottery, terra-cotta figurines, carved stonework, bronze weapons, metalwork, jewelry, and dyed textiles. Trading routes by land and sea extended to what are now Iraq, Iran, Afghanistan, and southern India. However, by 1500 B.C.E. the Indus Valley civilization had collapsed. It may have declined as a result of catastrophic floods, climate change, or over-intensive agriculture, and it was easy prey for foreign invaders. However, civilization continued to thrive to the east, on the plains of the Ganga (GAHN-guh) River (now in India).

The Aryan Culture

From 1500 B.C.E. onward there were waves of invasions by peoples known today as Aryans (AHR-yuhns) or Indo-Europeans. They entered the Punjab region from Persia (PER-zhuh: now Iran) and eradicated what remained of the Indus Valley cities. The land that is now Pakistan (PAK-ih-stahn) was occupied by a number of separate Aryan tribes.

By 600 B.C.E. Aryan culture had already swept on beyond the Sutlej (SUHT-lehj)

Collapse of Indus Valley civilization; Aryan invasions	Parts of Pakistan under Persian rule	Alexander the Great defeats King Porus
1500 B.C.E.	**546 B.C.E.**	**326 B.C.E.**

River to the plains of the Ganga. That region became the center of the Hindu religion and saw the stratification of society into social classes known as castes. This era of the subcontinent's history is known as the Vedic (VAE-dihk) period, after the ancient Hindu hymns known as Vedas (VAE-duhz), which were composed between 1500 and 1000 B.C.E.

Empires and Invaders

In the sixth century B.C.E. a powerful empire developed in Persia, and by 546 B.C.E. it extended from what is now Turkey in the west to Pakistan in the east. The Persian King Darius I, who came to the throne in 522 B.C.E., probably ruled over the north of Pakistan and parts of Sind and the Punjab. During his reign there were several wars between the Greeks and Persians, and soldiers from the Indus Valley region were sometimes drafted (called up to fight in the Persian army).

In 336 B.C.E. a Greek army, led by the young Macedonian (ma-seh-DOE-nee-uhn) ruler Alexander the Great, invaded Asia and overthrew the Persian Empire. Alexander crossed the Hindu Kush (HIHN-doo KUSH) and advanced to the Jhelum (JAH-lehm) River, where in 326 B.C.E. he defeated the army of King Porus, who ruled the region between the Jhelum and Chenab (cheh-NAWB) Rivers. Alexander then advanced to the Beas (BEE-aws) River (now in India), but his soldiers were weary

The Shrine of the Double-Headed Eagle at Taxila is part of a Buddhist monument dating from the first century B.C.E. It combines traditional Asian and Greek design.

and refused to march any farther. They turned south to the coast and then headed for home. Alexander died during this journey, in 323 B.C.E. Sikander (a form of Alexander) remains a name given to Pakistani boys to this day.

A Macedonian governor of Babylonia (bab-ih-LOE-nee-yuh) called Seleucus I came to rule Persia in 312 B.C.E., and Greek (Hellenistic) culture began to spread across the southwestern quarter of the Asian continent. However, Seleucus was unable to maintain rule over the Indus Valley, which in 300 B.C.E. was ceded to the Mauryan (MAWR-yahn) Empire of India. The greatest of the Mauryan emperors was Asoka (ruled ca. 265–238 B.C.E.), who made Buddhism the state religion of his realm. He built a stupa (SHTOO-pah: a religious monument) at Taxila (TAK-sih-lah), near modern Islamabad (ihz-LAH-muh-bad).

In around 200 B.C.E. much of Mauryan Pakistan fell to a king of Greek descent,

Indus Valley becomes part of Mauryan Empire	Rule by Bactrian Greeks	Saka invasions
300 B.C.E.	ca. **200** B.C.E.	ca. **100** B.C.E.

315

Gandharan Art

The Peshawar region, known as Gandhara (guhn-DAWR-ah), gave its name to a brilliant artistic tradition that reached its peak under Kushan rule in the second century C.E. Gandharan art includes stone sculptures, stucco reliefs, and reliquaries (shrines or containers in which sacred artifacts are kept). It combines the styles and motifs of the Indian subcontinent with traditional Greek styles, first imported into the region with the armies of Alexander the Great. The subject matter includes figures of the Buddha and Buddhist monks. They may be shown wearing Asian-style clothing, but the representation of the folds in the cloth is very much in the Greek manner. Gandharan sculpture is marked by grace and simplicity, but the stuccowork is generally more lively and personal than the rather stylized statues.

Demetrius, who came from Balkh (BAHLK: also known as Bactria) in Afghanistan. The culture of his kingdom, with its capital at Taxila, was a mixture of Greek (Hellenistic) and Asian influences. It reached its height in the second century B.C.E. under a wise king called Menander (or Milinda), who adopted the Buddhist faith. However, the kingdom soon fragmented into rival states.

In the first century B.C.E. these states were overrun from the north by waves of Saka (SAH-kuh) and then by Parthians (PAHR-thee-uhnz) from Persia. In the first century C.E. the Kushan (KOO-shahn), nomads from the borders of China, swarmed into Pakistan and became overlords of the Saka and Parthian populations. The greatest Kushan ruler was called Kanishka. Kanishka was a builder of Buddhist monuments and towns in the second century. His capital was at Peshawar (PEHSH-uh-wahr).

In the third century the Kushan Empire broke up, with incursions from the Persians in the west and from central Asian nomads in the north. In the fifth and the sixth centuries the warlike White Huns burst into Pakistan and northern India, as did other invaders, such as the Gurjaras (GOOR-zhah-rahz), and formed new kingdoms in the region.

The Coming of Islam

After 661 a Muslim Arab dynasty known as the Umayyad (OO-mie-yahd) Caliphate conquered vast areas of Spain, northern Africa, the Middle East, and central Asia. The Umayyad Arabs also subdued Persia and reached what is now southern Pakistan

Kushan rule	White Hun invasions	Umayyad Arab invasion of south
ca. 100 C.E.	ca. 400s–500s	711

in 711, when a large army with six thousand cavalry invaded the region. It was commanded by a young general named Muhammad bin Qasim.

However, Umayyad power was now overstretched, and although Muslim Arabs held on to Baluchistan, Sind, and parts of the Punjab, they soon lost control of northern Pakistan to Hindu kingdoms. Nevertheless, Islamic control was reestablished when Mahmud of Ghaznī, a Turkish ruler of Afghanistan, conquered the north and parts of the south in the year 1000. From now on the faith of Islam would play the leading role in the religion and politics of the region. Ghaznavid (GAHZ-neh-vihd) dominance of Pakistan lasted until 1187, when the ruling line was overthrown by Muhammad of Ghor.

From 1206 a series of Muslim dynasties ruled most of northern India and Pakistan from Delhi (DEHL-lee) in India, suffering repeated attacks by Mongol invaders in the thirteenth century and from the Mongol and Turkish armies of Temür (Tamerlane) in the late 1300s.

The Mughal Empire

It was Bābur, a Muslim from central Asia and a descendant of Temür, who in 1526 founded the Mughal (MOO-gahl) Empire, which ruled much of the Indian subcontinent, including Pakistan.

A depiction of Shah Jahan, Lahore's most famous son. He became Mughal emperor in 1628 after a revolt against his father. Thirty years later his sons rebelled against him.

Memorable successors included Akbar the Great (1542–1605), who was born in Umarkot (OO-mawr-kawt), Sind; Shah Jahan (1592–1666), who was born in Lahore (luh-HOER), and his son Aurangzeb (1618–1707), born in Dohad (DOE-huhd), in India.

The Mughal Empire at its greatest extent was a remarkable feat of administration,

Conquest by Mahmud of Ghaznī	Muhammad of Ghor overthrows Ghaznavids	Bābur founds Mughal Empire
1000	1187	1526

Mughal Lahore

The Mughal emperors commissioned some of the world's most beautiful and celebrated buildings. Fine examples of such architecture may be seen in the city of Lahore, which Akbar the Great made his capital.

- ***Shahi Qila*** *(shuh-HEE kee-LAH), Lahore's famous royal fort, was completed in 1566, during the reign of Akbar the Great. It was added to by later emperors and includes palaces, gardens, reception halls, pavilions, mosques, and a palace of mirrors.*

- *The **Tomb of the Emperor Jahangir** at Lahore dates from 1637. It was designed by his beloved wife, Nur Jahan, and built by his son, Shah Jahan, using sandstone and marble.*

- *The magnificent and very large **Badshahi** (buhd-SHAH-hee) **Mosque** in Lahore was completed in 1674, during the reign of Aurangzeb. It has three marble domes and four soaring minarets (the towers from which the faithful are called to prayer) constructed of sandstone.*

and is remembered especially for its artistic achievements. Small jewel-like Mughal paintings (known as miniatures) bring together Persian and Indian styles in scenes of court life and hunting.

The British Empire

The Mughal Empire weakened in the eighteenth century, and its hold over the Indian subcontinent was increasingly challenged by European powers such as the British and French. Mughal possessions in the northwest were seized by Persians in the 1730s; by the Afghans, who took control of Sind; and by the Sikhs of the Punjab who formed their own empire. The ashes of the great Sikh leader Ranjit Singh (1780–1839) are honored at a shrine in Lahore.

Meanwhile, the British East India Company, an armed commercial organization backed by the British government, had become the virtual ruler of the subcontinent and wanted control of

The magnificent Badshahi Mosque, opposite Lahore's royal fort, is one of the finest buildings in Pakistan. It dates back to the prosperous reign of the Mughal emperor Aurangzeb.

Decline of Mughal Empire; Persian and Sikh incursions	British war with Afghanistan	British take Sind	British take Punjab from the Sikhs
1730s–1800s	**1839**	**1843**	**1849**

the northwest too. In 1839 Britain went to war with the Afghans to gain control of the far northwest. Under the command of Sir Charles Napier, the British won Sind at the Battle of Hyderabad (hie-DEH-ruh-bad) in 1843 and by 1849 had taken the Punjab from the Sikhs.

In 1857 native troops rose up against British rule, but were suppressed. As a result, the whole subcontinent came under the direct rule of the British government. Although the revolt had begun among the Hindus, the British suspected Muslims were plotting to bring back Mughal rule and began to exclude them from responsible positions, causing resentment and, consequently, a strengthening of Islamic fervor.

The often lawless North-West Frontier Province (NWFP) lay below the Khyber (KIE-buhr) Pass, a mountainous route that still leads into Afghanistan. This area proved very difficult for Britain, then the

Rail transportation is one of the more lasting reminders of British rule in Pakistan. This photograph shows a railroad crossing the plain of the Punjab near Lahore in around 1880.

world's most powerful nation, to control, even with their modern forts. It was, however, believed to be of great strategic interest, for the Russians were advancing into central Asia and Britain feared for its interests in the region. War with the Afghans broke out twice more in 1878 and yet again in 1919.

Under British rule railroads were built and canals were dug to irrigate the western Punjab and the northern Indus Valley. This increased yields of wheat and cotton and brought in new settlers from the east.

In 1885 British India's subjects, Hindu and Muslim alike, founded the Indian National Congress to campaign for political freedom. However, in 1906 the Muslims broke away to found their own group, the All-India Muslim League. In 1916 the two groups agreed to work together, but by

Uprising against British	War between British and Afghans in northwest Pakistan	Founding of Indian National Congress	All-India Muslim League founded
1857	**1878**	**1885**	**1906**

1930 a leading nationalist, the poet Sir Muhammad Iqbal (1877–1938), was already calling for a separate Muslim state in northwestern India.

Independence and Partition

The leading Muslim politician in the independence movement was Mohammed Ali Jinnah (1876–1948). Initially he had supported cooperation between Hindus and Muslims, but in the 1930s he took the Muslim League on a separatist course.

In 1947, after World War II (1939–1945), the British agreed to Jinnah's demands, and when independence came, India was divided into two states. The new nation of

Karachi-born Mohammed Ali Jinnah in 1943. Jinnah was chiefly responsible for the creation of a separate Pakistani nation when India gained its independence.

Pakistan was itself to comprise two sections, each geographically separated from the other. In the northwest was West Pakistan (today's Pakistan), while in the far northeast was East Pakistan (the state known today as Bangladesh).

The Hindu ruler of a state called Jammu and Kashmir (JUHM-oo and KASH-meer: commonly known as Kashmir) decided to pledge his land to India, despite the fact that a majority of Kashmiris (kahsh-MEER-eez) were Muslims. This led to decades of violence and warfare, poisoning relations between the two new countries. People expected partition to be difficult, but few envisioned the bloodbath that ensued as Hindus fled from Pakistan to India and Muslims from India to Pakistan. Between half a million and a million people were killed in ethnic violence, and some fourteen million became refugees.

Troubled Times

Jinnah died in 1948, and his successor, Liaquat Ali Khan, was assassinated in 1951. The democratic National Assembly was abolished in 1954, and in 1956 Pakistan became an Islamic Republic. Its first president, Major General Iskandar Mirza, abolished political parties in 1958 and was himself overthrown in a military coup led by the prime minister, Mohammad Ayub Khan. The army continued to play a dominant role in Pakistan throughout the rest of the century. An inconclusive war broke out with India over Kashmir in 1965. Ayub Khan faced increasing political chaos, and was replaced by General Yahya

Second war between British and Afghans in northwest Pakistan	Muhammad Iqbal calls for separate Muslim state	Independence and partition: founding of Pakistan (East and West)
1919	**1930**	**1947**

Khan, who conceded free elections in December 1970.

Relations were bitter between East and West Pakistan, and the huge distance between them was not the only problem. Easterners felt that they were treated as second-class citizens in the new state, and in the election they voted for a separatist, Sheikh Mujibur Rahman (1920–1975). West Pakistan sent in troops and millions of East Pakistani refugees fled to India. In 1971 the conflict turned into a full-scale war, in which India intervened and defeated West Pakistan. East Pakistan became an independent state known as Bangladesh.

Many in Pakistan were embittered by the secession of the east, and there was a great deal of political tension. In 1977 Pakistan's leader, Zulfikar Ali Bhutto (1928–1979), was

East Pakistanis flee to the Indian border in December 1971, as they try to escape the fighting between Bangladeshi rebel forces and Pakistani government troops.

overthrown in a military coup staged by General Muhammad Zia-Ul-Haq. Bhutto was hanged in 1979. In the 1980s his daughter Benazir Bhutto campaigned for free elections, and after Zia-Ul-Haq's death in a plane crash in 1988, she was democratically elected as prime minister. However, she was in turn accused of corruption and forced out of office by President Ghulam Ishaq Khan.

The conservative Islamic Democratic Alliance now held power, led by Nawaz Sharif. However, he was forced to resign in 1993 along with President Khan following a bitter struggle for power between the two. Benazir Bhutto regained

Death of Mohammed Ali Jinnah	Pakistan becomes an Islamic Republic	Military coup by Ayub Khan	War with India over Kashmir
1948	**1956**	**1958**	**1965**

Neighbors and Rivals

At the border post of Wagah (wuh-GAH), to the east of Lahore, there is an extraordinary scene at the end of each day as Indian and Pakistani army officers each lower their respective flags and slam shut the iron gates that bar the road. Adorned in turbans and magnificent uniforms, each squad struts like fighting cocks in front of the crowd that gathers to watch and cheer. The soldiers stamp, shout, and sneer in a theatrical show of contempt for the other.

Nationalism is rife on both sides of the border, inflamed since partition by the conflicts over Kashmir and Bangladesh. The military display might be theater, but it does relate to genuine national divisions that pose dangers for the region and the world as a whole. In 1998 Pakistan demonstrated that it had developed advanced nuclear weapons to match those already owned by India. This news was met by public celebrations in Pakistan but anxiety among the international community.

Today, however, there is some hope that even if Kashmir remains an area of possible conflict (with Pakistan and India both controlling parts of the region), relations between the two hostile neighbors show some prospects of improving.

Indian (left) and Pakistani (right) guards perform the ritual closure of the border at Wagah. Recently relations between Pakistan and its larger neighbor seem to be improving.

office in October 1993, but following further allegations of corruption, Nawaz Sharif was reelected in 1997.

Pakistan Today

In October 1999 there was yet another miltary coup, bringing General Pervez Musharraf to executive power in place of Nawaz Sharif. Musharraf has since used a referendum and parliamentary support to secure his position as president and head of state until 2007, but he has failed to introduce democratic elections to the presidency, as promised. Despite this, and his development of nuclear weapons, he was adopted by the United States as a key ally in its ongoing military actions in

War with India; East Pakistan secedes as Bangladesh	Zulfikar Ali Bhutto overthrown by Zia-Ul-Haq	Benazir Bhutto becomes first female prime minister of Pakistan
1971	**1977**	**1988**

Pakistani women dress in colorful clothing. Head scarves, or dupiattas (doo-PYAH-tuhz), are often worn by women from many of the country's ethnic and religious groups.

western Asia since 2001. This alliance was opposed by radical Islamists within Pakistan.

Pakistan's parliament, or Majlis-e-Shoora (MAHZH-lees-eh-SHOO-ruh), has two chambers: the Senate and the National Assembly. The Senate is made up of one hundred representatives indirectly elected by regional assemblies. Elections were held in 2001 for the National Assembly, although opponents of Musharraf have attempted to disrupt proceedings since he came to power. The large number of political parties in Pakistan form many coalitions. One such alliance, the Pakistan Muslim League, is the largest party in parliament. Shaukat Aziz has held the office of prime minister since August 2004.

Pakistan's Ethnic Groups

The inhabitants of Pakistan are known as Pakistanis. They are descended from the many different peoples who have settled in the region since ancient times and vary considerably in appearance, from their features to the darkness of their skin. Linguists have identified sixty-six different languages in Pakistan and these, together with varying customs, religious affiliations, dress, and ways of life distinguish the different ethnic groups.

English, the language of administration during the period of the British Empire, is still widely spoken among the educated classes. The English language is valued in education, offering access to overseas universities and business schools. Immigration overseas, especially to Britain, has maintained the close historical ties with British culture.

Urdu and the Mohajir

The official language of Pakistan is Urdu, despite the fact that it is the mother tongue of around only 8 percent of the population. It is, however, spoken by many more educated Pakistanis as a second or third language, a means of communicating with other ethnic groups.

Urdu developed as a military and, later, literary language of the Mughal Empire, whose administrative language was Farsi

Pervez Musharraf ousts Nawaz Sharif	Pakistan becomes ally of United States	Shaukat Aziz becomes prime minister
1999	**2001**	**2004**

323

Speaking Urdu

Urdu is a member of the huge Indo-European language family, which extends from western Europe to northern India. It is closely related to Punjabi and is written in a Persian form of the Arabic script. It has borrowed or adapted many words from English, Farsi (Persian), and the many other languages it has encountered historically.

Asalaam aleikum *(uh-sah-LAHM uh-LAE-kuhm)*	*Hello (peace be with you)*
Aap kairyat se hai? *(AHP kier-YAHT suh HIE)*	*How are you?*
Kudaa haafiz *(KOO-duh HAH-fihz)*	*Goodbye*
Shukriyaa *(shuhk-REE-yuh)*	*Thank you*
jee haa *(zhih-HAH)*	*yes*
jee nahee *(jee-NAH-hee)*	*no*
ek, do, teen, char, panch *(AEK, DOE, TEEN, CHAHR, PAHNCH)*	*one, two, three, four, five*

who fled into Pakistan from India in 1947 and their descendants). Most Mohajir settled in Sind, where they make up around two-thirds of the population of Karachi (kuh-RAH-chee), the great southern port that was the national capital from 1947 to 1959. Mohajir play an important part in the administration and business life of Pakistan and the current president, Pervez Musharraf, belongs to this group.

In Sind

The Sind region takes in the eastern section of the Arabian Sea coast and the lower reaches of the Indus River. As Mohajir moved into Sind at partition in 1947, much of its Hindu population moved out, emigrating from Pakistan to India.

Today, alongside the Mohajir, live the various peoples who are native to the Sind region. Most are speakers of Sindhi (SIHND-hee), another Indo-European language, which is used officially in

Near Sukkur, in northern Sind, children help their father make bricks at a kiln. Many families are trapped in poverty and forced to work for rich landowners until they clear their debts.

(FAHR-see: Persian). Urdu has been associated with Pakistani nationalism since the days of the All-India Muslim League. Its imposition as an official language was resented in the old East Pakistan, where most of the population spoke Bengali, and this became a political issue that contributed to the secession of Bangladesh in 1971.

Most people who speak Urdu in modern Pakistan are Mohajir (moo-hah-JEER: the Muslim immigrants regional government administration. Sindhi-speakers make up around 12 percent of the national population. Famous Sindhis include the Bhutto family of politicians. Sindhi culture is rooted in thousands of years of agriculture, trade, and urban civilization. Its chief cities are Karachi, Hyderabad, Nawabshah, Shikarpur, and Sukkur, and the region is rich in music, literature, arts, and textile crafts.

The Sansi (SAN-see) of northwestern Sind are a poor people with little education, who often survive by begging. The Od (OED) are scattered across Sind and southern Punjab, many of them laboring in brickworks or as builders. Another ethnic group called the Bagri (BAH-gree) may be found living on the outskirts of some cities in Sind. They are part of a larger mobile population that moves back and forth across the Punjab region and Rajasthan (RAH-juh-stan) in India. They speak an Indo-European language, and some two hundred thousand are believed to live in Pakistan. The Dhatki (DAHT-kee) live in southeastern Sind, in the Tharparkar and Sanghar districts, and a people called the Koli (KOE-lee) form various groups, living as tenant farmers on the plains or raising herds in the Thar Desert.

Peoples of the Punjab

The Punjab region of the subcontinent takes in western and central Pakistan as well as part of northeastern India. The Pakistani Punjab extends from the northern capital, Islamabad, to Lahore in the east, and south to the confluence of the Indus tributaries.

Some 59 percent of Pakistanis identify themselves as Punjabis, and they have dominated the political and cultural life of Pakistan since independence. Many poor Punjabis live in small farming villages, growing crops on the irrigated plains.

The Punjabis are mostly descended from those Aryan tribes that remained in the region after the incursions of 3,500 years ago. Evidence of this lies in their traditional social structure, which is based on groups of common descent and

Women at Multan, in the Punjab, choose from hundreds of fancy textile designs before the celebration of a wedding. Multan is in a cotton-growing area.

Wearing the Salwar Kameez

While Western dress for men (for example, suits, shirts, and T-shirts) may be seen in cities, the majority of Pakistani men prefer to wear kameez *(kuh-MEEZ: loose cotton tunics) over* salwar *(SAHL-wahr: baggy pants), which are practical, durable, and in accordance with Islamic ideas of modest clothing. They may be white, gray, or beige. Men sometimes wear turbans, tied in various styles around the head, or round skullcaps. Formal wear for a wedding or political reception might include tailored white breeches called* churidars *(CHOO-rih-dahrz), a* sherwani *(shahr-WAH-nee: long, fitted jacket), and the fur cap made famous by Mohammed Ali Jinnah, the father of the Pakistani nation.*

Women's dress emphasizes Islamic ideals of modesty. Here too the salwar kameez (SAHL-wahr kuh-MEEZ: tunic and baggy pants) is worn, although it may be more tailored and made from more colorful or fine textiles than the male version. Sometimes the tunic is called a kurta *(KOOR-tuh). Hair is often braided into a long, single plait down the back, and a long scarf, or* dupiatta *(doo-PYAH-tuh), is worn to cover the head, and draped over the shoulders.*

Regional dress may vary considerably from the national norm. Kalasha (kuh-LAH-shuh) women are known for their multistranded bead necklaces and headdresses. In many areas of the north and northwest, especially among Pashtun (pahsh-TOON) men, a round felt hat with a rolled brim is popular. Among strict Pashtun Muslims, women may wear the full tentlike veil known as the burka (BUR-kah).

Female students in Lahore wear the traditional salwar kameez. Pakistan has had a female prime minister, but women still face discrimination in some sections of society.

profession known as *qaum* (KAWM). This is the equivalent to the caste system that developed among Aryans in northern India, but it is less rigid and lacks the religious implications given to that system by Hinduism. The Punjabi social structure encourages loyalty to the family and clan, or *biradari* (beer-uh-DAH-ree), and the ideal of mutual help and support. The clan chief is accorded great respect and often decides how clan members will vote and place their political allegiance.

The western form of the Punjabi language is the most common tongue in Pakistan and is also widely spoken by expatriate Pakistanis. It belongs to the Indo-European family and merges with neighboring languages and dialects such as Sindhi and Saraiki (sah-RIE-kee). Punjabi has a rich literary tradition. Indian languages such as Gujarati (goo-juh-RAH-tee) and Rajasthani (rah-juhs-THAH-nee) may also be heard across parts of the Punjab and Sind.

Baluchistan

Baluchistan (buh-LOO-kih-stan: sometimes spelled Balochistan) is a large but sparsely inhabited plateau region of rock and desert, where many of the inhabitants lead a hard life as herders. Most of the region's population lives in the area around the city of Quetta (KWEHT-tuh), which lies on the chief route between Iran and Pakistan.

The Baluchi (buh-LOO-chee: or Baluch) people live in Baluchistan and also along Pakistan's southwest coast, as well as over the borders of Iran and Afghanistan. In Pakistan their language, which is Indo-European and related to Pashtu (PAHSH-too), takes three main forms (eastern,

A Baluchi woman from southwestern Pakistan comes face to face with a camel from the herd. Many Baluchis still lead a nomadic or seminomadic existence.

western, and southern), with numerous dialects, and is written in the Urdu script. The old Baluchi way of life was seminomadic, as the tribes led their sheep to seasonal pastures. Today most Baluchis lead a more settled life as farmers, or else travel as migrant laborers. From 1973 to 1977 the Baluchis fought an unsuccessful separatist war against central government. The traditional structure of Baluchi society is centered upon the household of a feudal chief, or *hakim* (huh-KEEM), who has authority over a group of farmers, herders, tenants, and servants.

Other peoples living in Baluchistan include the Pashtun, Hazara (huh-ZAH-ruh), and smaller ethnic groups such as the Lasi- (LAH-se) speakers of the southeast and the Waneci- (wuh-NAE-see) speakers of the northeast. The Brahui (brah-HOO-ee) people live around Peshawar, Quetta, and Kalat (kuh-LAT), as well as in eastern Baluchistan and Sind. The fact that their language belongs to the Dravidian linguistic family of the earliest peoples of the subcontinent suggests that they may be descendants of the ancient Indus Valley civilization. The Brahui too have a history of nomadic herding, but they have leaned toward a more settled agricultural existence in recent times.

Heading North

The swathe of land that stretches northward from Baluchistan to Peshawar and on into the Hindu Kush is known as the North-West Frontier Province (NWFP). Much of it borders Afghanistan, and it has a large population of Afghan refugees who, over recent decades, have fled from a seemingly endless series of wars and natural disasters in that country. They include speakers of Dari (DAH-ree), the eastern form of Farsi (Persian), and Pashtu.

In 1969 the NWFP was extended to include the far northern regions of Dir

Gun Law

The chief ethnic group of the NWFP is the Pashtun, whose homeland extends over the border into Afghanistan. Pashtun men often carry guns and wear belts of ammunition, a tradition dating back to the nineteenth century. For many years they carried the antique rifles used in the wars against the British Empire. Today they may carry more modern weapons: copies of well-known makes, such as the Russian Kalashnikov, made by Pashtun gunsmiths. A small town to the south of Peshawar called Darra Adam Khel (DAH-ruh uh-DAHM KEHL), which is populated by the Adam khel (KEHL: clan), is famous as the center of this illicit manufacture. More than a hundred gunsmithing workshops in the main street turn out all sorts of pistols and automatic weapons. The finished products are smuggled past checkpoints to the rest of the NWFP and the Afghan borderlands.

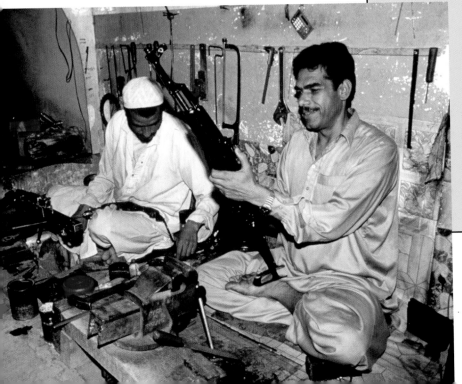

Traditional Pashtun metalworking skills find a market in the gun-toting culture of the North-West Frontier Province, where there are many illicit arms manufacturers.

The Kalasha

The Kalasha people live in the wooded mountain valleys of Birir (bih-REER), Bumboret (BUHM-boe-reht), and Rumbur (ROOM-boor), at the eastern end of the Hindu Kush range. They are related to the Nuristani (noor-ih-STAH-nee) people living across the border in Afghanistan. Their language is Indo-European and related to Farsi (Persian).

The Kalasha are a farming people. The men look after herds of goats and sheep, while the women cultivate crops such as millet and wheat. Kalasha homes, made of stone and carved wood, are set into the steep hillsides. Society is governed by a village chief known as a kazi (KAH-zee) and elders, whose rulings are administered by younger men called roi (ROY). The Kalasha have their own religion, believing in a number of gods and a supreme creator called Dezau, and so are sometimes termed Kafirs (kuh-FEERZ: "nonbelievers") by their Muslim neighbors. They celebrate the passing of the seasons with festivals and dancing. However, Kalasha traditions are threatened by the increase in tourism in the valleys.

The wooden housing of Kalasha villages is built on steep mountain valleys. With little space available, the multistory dwellings are built very close to each other.

(DEER), Swat (SWAHT), and Chitral (chih-TRAHL). Large areas of the NWFP are designated as tribal areas, which are administered by traditional chiefs called *maliks* (MAH-lihkz) in association with political agents appointed by the central government. There are also a number of smaller frontier regions under local administration. Public travel is restricted in many parts of the NWFP, and an armed escort is generally required for outsiders.

The Pashtun way of life is determined by Islam and follows ancient social customs. It is still governed by a very strict code of honor known as *Pashtunwali* (pahsh-toon-WAH-lee). This insists upon generosity and hospitality to strangers and on fair dealing. Anyone offending the honor of another with violence or personal insult may be subjected to vengeance by all those related to the victim. Feuds are often bitter and long lasting and may erupt into tribal warfare. The only means of settling such disputes is by referral to a council of tribal elders, which may decide upon compensation to be paid or some other penalty.

Many Pashtun homes resemble—and sometimes serve as—small forts with lookout towers. The traditional house is built of dried mud around a compound that has high walls and wooden gates and shutters. The walls serve as defenses and also screen the women of the house from public gaze. Pashtun society is very much male dominated; women do not venture out without being veiled. The compound is generally planted with trees that provide shade in the fierce heat of summer. Areas are set aside for prayers, cooking, storage, and for stables. Beds of wood and rope are used for sitting as well as for sleeping. Rooms lead directly on to the compound and are occupied by the head of the household and his extended family, and also include an all-important hall where guests are received and the men discuss business.

Traveling north into the Chitral and Swat districts, or eastward across the upper Indus, the Pashtun homeland gives way to the territories of smaller ethnic and linguistic groups such as the Chitralis (chih-TRAH-leez: also known as Khowars), the Kalamis (kuh-LAH-meez: also known as Kohistanis), the Torwalis (toer-WAH-leez), and the Wakhi (WAH-kee).

The Karakoram (kah-ruh-KOER-ahm) Highway is a rough, high-altitude road

The Burusho

Like other peoples living in remote mountain valleys, the Burusho (buh-ROO-shoe: also known as Hunzakuts) have long attracted all sorts of speculation and mythologizing by the outside world. They live in the Karakoram Mountains, in the region of Gilgit (GIHL-guht). It is said that they live extraordinarily long lives, but this has never been proved. It is true that their language, Burushkashi (buh-roosh-KAH-shee), is what linguists call an "isolate," which means that it is not related to any other known modern language. It is claimed that the Burusho are descended from the soldiers of Alexander the Great, and they certainly have a rather European appearance. They were ruled by a local dynasty from the Middle Ages until 1974 and follow the Ismaili (eesh-MAE-lee) form of Islam. Their lands have been opened up in recent years with the development of the Karakoram Highway.

A woman sits by the Neelum River with her granddaughter. She lives on the border between Pakistani- and Indian-controlled Jammu and Kashmir, which divides many families.

leading from Gilgit through the bleak mountains of Pakistan's Northern Areas into China. Here people herd yaks as well as goats and grow barley. The Gujar (goo-JAHR) people practice transhumance, a means of subsistence whereby they lead their herds to high mountain pastures during the summer months and return to the valleys in winter. Other northern peoples include the Shina (SHEE-nuh) and the Balti (BAHL-tee), whose language is a form of Tibetan.

The region of Jammu and Kashmir is a land of valleys, high mountains, and lakes. Its peoples include Gujar herders and speakers of Kashmiri (kahzh-MEER-ee). The region is renowned for its style of craftwork, which is said to be more than five hundred years old. Kashmiri women often make intricately embroidered clothing, particularly shawls, which are commonly worn during the cold winter months. Carpenters make wooden ornaments, often from the walnut trees that grow in this region. Baskets are made from willow rushes and used to carry goods to and from the bustling markets.

An Islamic Republic

Ninety-six percent of Pakistanis are Muslims. Friday is the chief day of worship, and Pakistan's towns and cities have a large number of imposing and historical mosques and holy sites. Islam was the reason for the Pakistani state's creation. The new nation was at first

dominated by a moderate approach to religion, but since the late 1970s there has been a growing current of Islamist fervor and political activity.

Men cleanse themselves before praying at a Muslim shrine in Lahore. The site commemorates the great Sufi thinker Data Ganj Bakhsh, who lived in the eleventh century.

Other Religions

Pakistan has constitutional commitments to religious freedom, and the national flag features not only the crescent emblem of Islam but also a white strip representing religious minorities. However, in practice, intolerance of small, unorthodox Islamic sects and also of people of other faiths is fairly common.

Only 4 percent of Pakistan's population is not Muslim. Around 1.6 percent is Christian, and churches from the British period may still be seen in cities. There is a small Hindu minority of about the same size, but many Hindus fled the country in

Branches of Faith

Seventy-six percent of Pakistanis follow the Sunni branch of Islam, while 20 percent are Shia Muslims. An offshoot of Shia is Ismaili Islam, and many Ismailis live in Pakistan's northern regions of Gojal (GOE-zhal) and the Hunza (HOON-zuh) Valley. Sufism is a mystical tradition of Islam that developed in the eighth century C.E. *and is acceptable to both Sunni and Shia*

Muslims. Sufi leaders are called pirs *(PEERZ). Sufis use various methods of meditation to achieve direct experience of God, and these include the repetition of God's name, whirling dances, poetry, music, singing, and clapping. The Sufi musical tradition of Pakistan and India is called* qawwali *(guh-WAH-lee) and was introduced by the composer Amir Khosrow (1253–1325).*

Water from the Indus

The people of the Indus Valley have always depended on the great river for their survival and livelihood. Throughout the last century the Indus River has increasingly been used for irrigation. Around 72 percent of the Indus River's flow is now taken for this purpose. The flow is diverted into a complex system of dams, reservoirs, canals, ditches, and watercourses. It is one of the greatest irrigation networks in the world. It is no exaggeration to say that this network makes it possible to provide enough food and water to keep Pakistan's population of more than 162 million alive; some 70,000 square miles (180,000 square kilometers) of farmland would turn to dust without it. However, the irrigation plan also creates environmental problems. Leakage and lack of proper drainage have resulted in waterlogged and salty soils in some areas, which cannot be cultivated. The great reduction in water flow through the Indus delta and the retention of silt by dams have prevented the natural expansion of the delta. Mangrove swamps, which protect coastal areas from flooding, are therefore at risk, as are stocks of fish and crustaceans that provide a livelihood for fishers.

1947. There are also small numbers of Sikhs and Buddhists, whose faiths played a major part in the history of the region. Karachi is home to a small community of Parsis (PAHR-sihs), a faith that originated in ancient Persia.

often forced into employment at an early age. Economic development has been hampered by corruption, political instability, and the constant threat of war with India. Recent years have seen anti-corruption campaigns and some recovery in

Making a Living

Pakistan is a land where the army holds great power, and political influence is also exerted by the Muslim clergy. Landowners and industrialists form a wealthy elite, and there is a middle class made up of merchants and traders. However, much of the population is very poor, and the country as a whole is underdeveloped. Children are

Children lead water buffalo from the fields. Farming has been a way of life on the fertile plains of the Punjab for at least five thousand years.

the Pakistani economy, but many Pakistanis still seek employment in the Middle East and Gulf states.

Around half of the workforce is employed on the land, many on small family holdings and tenant farms. Agriculture is centered around the plains of the Indus River. Around 28 percent of the country is suitable for cultivation. Wheat, corn, rice, lentils, vegetables, oilseeds, and sugarcane are important crops. Hardier cereal crops such as millet and barley are necessary in more marginal lands. The valleys of the northern mountains provide almonds, walnuts, apricots, mulberries, and cherries. The Quetta and Kalat districts of Baluchistan are known for their dates and fruit. Cotton is the chief fibrous crop and the country's most valuable export. Cattle, sheep, goats, and poultry are raised, and hides are used in leather manufacture. Fisheries and shrimp industries are important in coastal regions, as is forestry in the north.

Modern trucks and motor scooters mix with a horse-drawn cart on a noisy Karachi road. Note the elaborate and colorful decorations on many of the vehicles.

Pakistan's natural resources include water, used for hydroelectric power, and valuable fields of oil, natural gas, and coal. Useful mineral reserves include copper, silver, iron ore, gypsum, chromite, rock salt, and limestone.

Many of Pakistan's factories process foods produced on the farm, such as sugar and vegetable ghee (a kind of cooking oil). Yarn, textiles, garments, and furnishings are produced at cotton mills. Carpets and rugs, chemicals and fertilizers, steel, bicycles, sports goods, cement, and building materials are other important manufactured products.

Transportation and Communication

Pakistan has nearly 68,375 miles (110,040 kilometers) of paved highway in addition to its dusty, rough-surfaced roads. An expressway links the capital, Islamabad, with Lahore, and the national highway also connects Karachi with Lahore. One famous historical route is the Grand Trunk Road from Peshawar to Lahore, celebrated

Saddar is the main shopping district in central Karachi and has many bazaars, covered markets, modern stores, and street markets like this one.

in the writings of Rudyard Kipling (1865–1936), who vividly chronicled the days of the British Empire. The Karakoram Highway to China, built over spectacular mountain passes and through remote deserts, is a modern route that is associated with some of the ancient trading routes of the Silk Road.

Road transportation includes bicycles, cars, taxis, minibuses, modern buses, old buses, and trucks. In some parts of the country buses and trucks are festooned with lights or painted with colorful designs and pictures, or inscribed with religious texts. In the cities, horses and carriages known as *tongas* (TAWNG-gahz) may be hired, or the motorized rickshaws, small vehicles, or motorcycles adapted to carry passengers, which hurtle through the busy streets.

Pakistan has more than 4,800 miles (7,725 kilometers) of rail, of which 188 miles (around 300 kilometers) is electrified. International airlines fly to Islamabad, Lahore, and Karachi. The telecommunications system in Pakistan is improving to meet the demands of business and private customers. People with access to the Internet number around 1.5 million.

Pakistan has a varied output of printed and online newspapers, both national and regional, in Urdu and also in English. Coverage is varied in its political affiliations, and the government is less heavy-handed in its relations with the media than it was twenty years ago or more. The Associated Press of Pakistan is an official news agency. Radio and television stations are state owned, but there are also private and international outlets, including satellite and cable television networks.

Country and Town Life

The great majority of Pakistan's population lives in the countryside. Living conditions have changed little over the ages, with single story, flat-roofed, brick houses built around courtyards with farm wells and pumps, and village markets selling fruit and vegetables.

However, 34 percent of Pakistanis are town or city dwellers, and that proportion is growing rapidly. The urban way of life varies greatly from one city to another. The national capital, Islamabad, is a city of modern concrete buildings, apartments, offices, hotels, and embassies. It was built from the 1960s onward, near the old town of Rawalpindi (raw-wuhl-PIN-dee). The city is designed on a grid pattern, in which each square is assigned a letter and number.

Peshawar and Quetta, however, are very different towns, retaining the atmosphere of the old imperial frontier, with bustling bazaars (markets), old forts, houses, verandas, open-fronted shops, courtyards, and mazes of streets. Lahore is different again; a large, sprawling city whose center still has grand public buildings and avenues dating from the days of the British Empire, a mixture of Victorian and imitation Mughal styles, and twentieth-century apartment buildings, railroad tracks, and crowded bazaars. Lahore is the cultural capital of the country, a center of music, art, poetry, and movies. Karachi remains the commercial center and largest seaport, another huge city of offices and markets.

Pakistani Dishes

Much Pakistani cooking has come from the Mughal tradition and has links with Iran, the Middle East, and central Asia. Many dishes and cooking methods are shared with northern India, but some have specific origins in Pakistan. One example of the latter is the tandoori (tahn-DOO-ree) style of cooking, which takes its name from the clay oven, fired by wood or charcoal, found in the courtyards of homes in the NWFP.

Rice is a common staple of the Pakistani diet. Typical of the Mughal cooking style

Flat Breads

Wheat is one of Pakistan's staple foods, and is made into a wide variety of breads, or rotis (ROE-teez).

- ***Naan** (NAHN) is a bread popular in Iran, Afghanistan, and Pakistan, cooked in the tandoori style of the NWFP. It forms a large, flat, thick, doughy oval pancake.*

- ***Chapatis** (chuh-PAH-teez) are thin, circular pancake breads, cooked on a griddle. They are made with whole wheat flour.*

- ***Parathas** (puh-RAH-thahz) are the same shape as chapatis and are also made of whole wheat flour. They are covered with ghee (a kind of cooking oil) before being fried on a griddle.*

- ***Puris** (POOR-eez) are small breads of whole wheat flour that puff up when deep fried.*

A street kitchen dishes up parathas, a kind of fried chapati, fresh from the griddle. The bread is covered in ghee, an important ingredient of south Asian cooking.

is pilaf (PEE-lahf), long-grained rice cooked in stock and flavored with spiced vegetables or meat. Plain boiled rice is called *sadha chaval* (SAH-duh shah-VAHL). *Biryani* (beer-YAH-nee) is a delicious steamed rice dish mixed with meat or vegetables. Popular vegetables include

After an early start, cart drivers in Peshawar sit on the ground in the shade to take a break. They share their breakfast of lentils (dal) and spices.

Boti Kebab

Boti kebab (BOE-tee kuh-BAWB) is marinated meat, grilled or barbecued on a skewer. Variants of the kebab are eaten all the way from Greece and Turkey eastward through Iran and Afghanistan to Pakistan. The following recipe serves six.

You will need:

2 lb (1 kilogram) diced lamb
¾ cup (180 milliliters) yogurt
1 tbsp (15 grams) ground coriander seeds
1 tbsp (15 grams) chopped coriander leaves
1 tsp (5 grams) salt
½ tsp (2.5 grams) hot chili powder
1 tbsp (15 grams) chopped root ginger
2 cloves of garlic, crushed
1 tsp (5 grams) turmeric
2 lemons

Mix all the herbs and spices together with the yogurt in a large basin. Add the diced lamb and stir until all pieces are well covered with the yogurt mixture. Leave in a refrigerator for 6 hours. Remove and skewer the diced lamb pieces, then grill or barbecue them. Garnish with wedges of the lemons. The kebabs may be served with rice or salad.

spinach, potatoes, peas, tomatoes, cauliflower, okra, and onions. Lentils, or dal (DAHL), are often stewed into a thick sauce. Yogurt, or *dahi* (DAH-ee: curd), is also a common dish and cooking ingredient.

Muslims do not eat pork. The most common meats eaten in Pakistan are lamb and chicken, but beef may also be served. Seafoods, including fish and prawns, are popular. All are cooked according to a variety of techniques, such as *do pyaaza* (doep-YAH-zuh: with lots of onions), *karai* (kuh-RIE: braised with vegetables), or *jalfrezi* (zhal-FREE-zee: with chilies and tomatoes). These dishes have become famous internationally because expatriate Pakistanis have opened restaurants in towns and cities throughout the world. Tropical fruits from southern Pakistan include mangoes, bananas, papayas, and melons. Desserts include a sort of pistachio-flavored ice cream called *kulfi* (KOOL-fee) and *keer* (KEER: rice pudding).

Street snacks include *pakoras* (puh-KOE-ruhz: battered, deep-fried vegetables) and samosas (suh-MOE-sahz: triangular parcels of pastry filled with meat or vegetables). Candy shops offer a colorful variety of confectionery, made with sugar, syrup, carrots, fruit, pistachio nuts, or condensed milk. Candy is often given as a gift when visiting the house of a friend.

Strong liquor may be produced by some ethnic minorities in the north, but most Muslims do not drink alcohol. Tea, however, is drunk everywhere in Pakistan, and is generally brewed together with milk and sugar. In the north and northwest, green teas may be drunk, sometimes flavored with cardamom seeds. *Lassi* (LAH-see), a milky beverage made from yogurt and iced water, is served either sweet or salty with cumin flavoring, and is popular with meals. Other beverages include mango and lime juice.

A splendidly dressed Pakistani bride and groom take part in a mass wedding ceremony in Lahore in July 2004. The event was arranged for poor families by the local authorities.

Society and Welfare

Men generally dominate the Pakistani social structure. Women may have influence within the home, but men tend to assume the role of breadwinner and head of household. In more liberal circles, however, women may be permitted to work. Marriages are normally arranged by families with a view to improving the material prospects of the family or forming socially acceptable alliances. The couple getting married may be strangers to each other, brought together by a relative, who acts as a matchmaker, or by a commercial agency. The bride's parents are expected to provide a dowry, a sum of money or a costly gift, to the new couple. Expectations can be very difficult to meet and sometimes result in arguments between the families. Households are traditionally extended, meaning that grandparents, parents-in-law, aunts, and uncles all play an important part in everyday family life.

Pakistan has a high birthrate but also a high rate of infant mortality, with eighty-five of every one thousand children dying before their first birthday. Life expectancy at birth is 60 years for males and 62 years for females. Common illnesses include diseases carried by mosquitoes, such as malaria and dengue fever; respiratory diseases, such as tuberculosis; and waterborne infections, such as typhoid and diarrhea. There is a shortage of doctors and hospital care outside the towns and cities.

Education starts with five years of elementary school and may continue with three years of middle school, which offers a general or vocational qualification. Two years of high school are necessary for

338

entrance to the universities or colleges of higher education. The social system favors the education of boys from wealthier classes of society. Poor children rarely have the opportunity to improve their situation through education. Sixty percent of males and only 31 percent of females over 15 years of age are able to read and write.

Poetry and Music

The chief literary medium of Pakistan is poetry, which is written in Urdu as well as most of the region's other major languages. A lasting influence is the Mughal tradition, in which love and beauty are constant themes. The classical love lyric is the *ghazal* (guh-ZAHL), a form of verse that originated in medieval Persia, often consisting of a dozen or so couplets. Other poetic themes over the ages have been inspired by Sufi mysticism, by folktales,

A poet and scholar, Allamah Nasir al-Din Nasir Hunzai (born 1917) contemplates the lines of a new poem. His poetry is written in the Burushkashi language of the Hunza region.

Nusrat Fateh Ali Khan

Nusrat Fateh Ali Khan (1948–1997) was the greatest modern performer of qawwali, the Sufi devotional music that has such a large following in Pakistan. He became known as "the Brightest Star." Qawwali is performed by singers accompanied by a small hand-pumped reed organ and dholak *(DOE-lahk) or* tabla *(TAH-bluh), both of which are double drums, the former played with fingers, the latter with the flat of the hand. It involves long improvised musical breaks.*

Nusrat's father was a famous performer of Pakistani classical music and came from a long line of musicians. Nusrat began singing in 1965, learning his skills from his uncles, with whom he performed before leading his own group of players from 1971.

Nusrat, a large man, had a magnificent voice and was recognized for his musical genius as well as his ability to reach popular audiences. His religious music, often performed at Sufi shrines, was inspired, but he also took on secular and popular themes and was never afraid to modernize and adapt. By the 1990s he had a worldwide following, collaborating with a wide range of Western musicians. Sadly, he died of liver failure at the age of 49.

and in the twentieth century by politics and human rights. Poetry is very much a living tradition, with the form of public poetry reading known as *mushaira* (moo-SHIE-ruh) as popular today as ever and attracting an international audience.

Dance can be a part of all kinds of celebrations in Pakistan, religious or secular. These colorful dancers are making a political point, supporting the Pakistan Muslim League.

The region's classic poets include the Punjabi Bulleh Shah (1680–1758), the Sindhi Shah Abdul Latif Bhitai (1689–1752) and the Pashtun Abdul Rahman Baba (1651–1710). Their work still inspires musicians today, for, as in many parts of the Middle East, the line between poetry and music is hard to draw.

Pakistani music takes many forms. There is qawwali, the Sufi music played in concerts as well as at smaller domestic gatherings, or *mahfils* (muh-FEELZ). Qawwali is only performed by men. There is classical music, in the same mode as that of India, having come from the court of the Mughal emperors. There is folk music performed by both men and women, which has fed its influence into modern pop music fusing Western and Eastern influences.

Dance has developed out of the folk traditions of Pakistan's various ethnic groups. Strict Muslims among the Pashtun may frown on dance as entertainment, but there is a strong Pashtun community tradition of large circle dances in which men brandish swords or guns.

Punjabi folk dances include *bhangra* (BAHNG-grah), originally a harvest festival stomp to the beat of a large drum, or *dhol* (DOEL). From there it moved to the cities, accompanied by smaller drums, simple fiddles, zithers, and flutes, and later by guitars and saxophones. Finally bhangra resurfaced on the other side of the world, among British Asians in the 1980s and 1990s, where its beat developed into highly charged electric dance music popular with young people of all ethnic groups.

340

Arts and Crafts

The marvelous historical traditions of Mughal painting and Islamic calligraphy still influence Pakistani arts and crafts today. For example, their intricacy and precision can be seen in the work of the woodcarvers, jewelers, and metalworkers who supply bazaars throughout Pakistan. Among the raw materials used are silver, gold, brass, copper, lacquer, precious stones, and fine walnut woods. Ivory was once common but is now a protected substance and has largely been replaced by bone.

While furnishings and garments are mass-produced in Pakistani factories, the traditional spinning wheel and loom still produce handwoven textiles, some coarse and practical, others fine and luxurious.

A potter in Peshawar puts the finishing touches on a teapot before placing it with the collection of dishes and vases for sale on his workshop shelf.

Phulkari Embroidery

A specialty of Punjabi women is a form of traditional embroidery called phulkari *(pool-KAH-ree: "flower work"). It is chiefly used to make shawls and employs a form of satin stitch that is worked into the surface of the cloth. The stitching is used both vertically and horizontally, which results in a variation in the texture of the finished shawl. Bold geometrical patterns, such as triangles, squares, and crosses, are common and are often produced in yellows, golds, reds, and creams. The densest embroidery work covers most of the base material, to make a shawl worn only for festivals and special occasions. This is called a* bagh *(BAHG) and is traditionally made by a woman on the birth of a granddaughter. It will be worn at her wedding and kept in the family as an heirloom.*

Silk is woven in Sind, cotton in the Punjab, and wool in the far north. Textile arts include tapestry weaving (a specialty of Multan), patchwork, appliqué, embroidery, mirror work (mirrors sewn into textiles), dyeing, and block printing. Products include bedcovers and quilts, cloth for turbans, kurtas (tunics), and shawls.

Pakistani rugs are mostly woven, but knotted carpets in both the Persian and Turkish tradition are also made. The Baluchi people are among the great carpet makers of Asia, although their best-known work comes from across the

(including the famous names Hashim and Jahangir).

The most popular sport in Pakistan, however, is cricket, introduced by the British in the nineteenth century. This bat-and-ball game, with eleven players on each side, is a national passion in Pakistan, its finer points being a favorite topic of conversation at all levels of society. Cricket is not just a spectator sport, but also a game for poor city boys on any backstreet or vacant lot. Pakistan's team plays cricket with consummate skill, and international games are occasions for celebration and highly charged emotion. Cricket stars are treated like heroes, and one of the best known players, Imran Khan (born in 1952), used his fame to launch a political career after his retirement from the game in 1992. In 2004 the arrival of an Indian national cricket team to play in Pakistan gave rise to hopes that the frosty relations between the two countries might be about to thaw.

Polo is another game formalized by the British, but its origins go back to ancient Persia. It is still played with enthusiasm in Pakistan, especially in the north of the country. It is a fast game played on horseback, with long mallets used to hit the ball. Afghan immigrants play a much wilder horseback game in the NWFP, with each team trying to seize the carcass of a dead goat from the other. The game is called *buzkashi* (boosh-KAH-shee), which means "goat grabbing."

border in Iran and central Asia. Leather is tooled and stitched to produce wallets, belts, purses, and slippers. Camel hide is also used in making lampshades and other souvenirs.

Basketry and the production of ceramic vessels and tiles are both popular and practical crafts with an ancient history in Pakistan. The regions of Bahawalpur (buh-HAH-wuhl-poor) and Cholistan (CHOE-lih-stan) produce a very thin black pottery, while Multan is known for its blue and white glazes.

Bat and Ball

Squash is a sport in which Pakistan has been a world champion since independence. The high-speed game has been dominated for many decades by one brilliant Pakistani squash "dynasty," the Khan family

Kabaddi (kuh-BAH-dee) is an ancient game unique to the subcontinent, being played in Pakistan as well as in India, Nepal, Bangladesh, and Sri Lanka. Two teams try to win points by touching or "capturing" their opponents while holding their breath. (To prove this, they must keep saying "Kabaddi" without stopping.) The result is somewhat like a game of tag mixed with wrestling.

Festivals

The religious calendar of Islam, the dates of which vary according to phases of the moon, dominates the Pakistani year with solemn and mournful events as well as with celebrations. The month of Ramadan, with fasting during daylight hours, ends with Eid ul-Fitr (EED uhl-FEET-ruh), a public holiday marked by the exchange of gifts and feasting.

Sufi pilgrims visit shrines of their saints on the *urs* (OORZ) or anniversary of their deaths, and there are festivals of qawwali in their honor. Lahore's Mela Cheraghan (MAE-luh sheh-RAH-gahn: Festival of Lights) celebrates the seventeenth-century Sufi mystic Shah Hussain. Farmers, peasants, and holy men come from all over the Punjab at the end of March to visit his mausoleum beside the famous Shalimar Gardens.

Spring Festival

Lahore's spring festival, Basant (buh-SAHNT: also known as Jashen Bahran), is celebrated in February or March each year. It is an ancient festival that has become increasingly popular in recent years, attracting visitors from other parts of the country. Basant is celebrated with feasting, music, dance, arts and crafts, and the wearing of yellow costumes or scarves, a symbol of the new spring. The most striking feature of the festival is kite flying. Thousands of kites of all shapes, sizes, and colors fill the skies and soar from parks and city roofs. At night, music rings out while white kites are flown, which reflect lights and fireworks.

Throughout Pakistan there are local spring fairs with folk dancing; feasting; fairground attractions, such as swings and ferris wheels (sometimes made of wood in rural areas); music; and sporting contests.

On the eve of the Basant spring festival, inhabitants of the city of Lahore go shopping for new kites, the more colorful the better.

Glossary

aid agency an association that provides people with help, such as water and food, in times of need.

alliance two or more people, organizations, or countries working together with the same aims.

archipelago a group or chain of islands; a wide stretch of water with many scattered islands.

cholera a serious and often fatal disease caused by the consumption of infected food or water.

clan a group of peoples who share a common ancestor.

coalition a temporary union between two or more groups.

colony a territory that is ruled by another country.

communist a believer in communism, a theory that suggests that all property belongs to the community and that work should be organized for the common good.

constitution a written statement outlining the laws of a country, stating people's rights and duties and establishing the powers and duties of the government.

coup a brilliant, sudden, and usually highly successful act, particularly the violent overthrow of an existing government by a small group.

delta the land at the mouth of a river where the river splits into several smaller streams.

democracy a state ruled by the people; a state in which government is carried out by representatives elected by the public.

dialect a nonstandard version of a language, such as one spoken in a particular region or by a particular group of people.

dynasty a ruling family.

enterprise a new, often risky, project.

expatriate somebody who has left their homeland to live or work in another country.

fertilizer a substance added to soil to increase its ability to support plant growth.

heirloom a piece of personal property handed down from generation to generation within a family.

heritage the traditions, status, and character acquired by being born into a particular family or social class, or something passed down from one generation to the next.

human rights rights that are considered by society to belong automatically to everyone.

hydroelectric of or relating to production of electricity from waterpower. The force of a waterfall or dammed river may be used to produce electricity in a power station.

immigrate to enter a country, seeking to live there.

immunization treatment (as with a vaccine) to produce immunity to a disease.

imperial of or relating to an empire.

incense a spicy substance that is burned to create a sweet smell, especially during religious services.

irrigate to supply land with water brought through pipes or ditches.

lacquer a material, such as a varnish, that dries quickly into a shiny layer.

leprosy an infectious disease that attacks the skin and nerves and can cause deformities and loss of sensation, weight, and strength.

linguist somebody who speaks several languages.

mangrove any of various tropical trees or shrubs that grow roots and form dense masses in salty marshes or shallow saltwater.

Middle East the countries of southwest Asia and northeast Africa—usually thought to include the countries extending from Libya in the west to Afghanistan in the east.

migrant somebody who moves from one place to another in search of work or economic opportunities.

missionary somebody sent to another country by a church to spread its faith or to do social and medical work.

monsoon a wind in the Indian Ocean and southern Asia that blows from the southwest from April to October and from the northeast from October to April.

nationalism a loyalty or devotion to a country; the promotion of policies designed to benefit or support a particular nation.

natural resource a natural material, such as coal or wood, that can be exploited by people.

nomadic describes people who do not have a permanent home but instead move from place to place, usually in search of pasture for their animals.

peninsula a piece of land sticking out from the mainland into a sea or lake.

pilgrim a person who travels to a shrine or holy place to worship.

plateau a broad flat area of high land.

protectorate a country or region that is protected by another, more powerful country.

rebel somebody who fights against his or her own government in order to change the political system.

referendum a vote in which all the people in a country are officially asked whether they agree with an important policy or proposal.

reform to make better by the removal of faults.

republic a country that has a president rather than a king or queen.

revolt to rise up against authority, usually a government.

ritual a traditional or routine ceremony.

secular not religious.

separatist a person who favors separation from a religious group, country, or an organization or group of any sort.

settlement a place where people have settled and built homes.

subtropical of, relating to, or being the regions bordering the tropical zone.

tsunami a great sea wave produced by a volcano eruption or earthquake under the sea.

tuberculosis an infectious disease caused by a bacterium and usually marked by weight loss, fever, coughing, and difficulty breathing.

United Nations an alliance, founded in 1945, that today includes most of the countries in the world. Its aim is to encourage international cooperation and peace.

waterborne supported, carried, or transmitted by water.

World War II a war that began in Europe in 1939 and spread to involve many other countries worldwide. It ended in 1945. The United Kingdom, France, the Soviet Union, the United States, Canada, Australia, New Zealand, and other European countries fought against Germany, Italy, and Japan.

zither a musical instrument, usually played with pick and fingers, consisting of a flat, shallow, horizontal sound box with up to forty-five metal strings stretched across it.

Further Reading

Internet Sites
Look under Countries A to Z in the Atlapedia Online Web Site at
    http://www.atlapedia.com
Use the drop-down menu to select a country on the CIA World Factbook Web Site at
    http://www.odci.gov/cia/publications/factbook
Locate "Choose a Country Profile," then use the drop-down menu to select a country at the
    Library of Congress Country Studies Web Site at
    http://lcweb2.loc.gov/frd/cs/cshome.html
Use the Country Locator Maps in the World Atlas Web Site at
    http://www.worldatlas.com/aatlas/world.htm
Look under the alphabetical country listing using the Infoplease Atlas at
    http://www.infoplease.com/countries.html
Use the drop-down menu to select a country using CountryReports.org at
    http://www.emulateme.com
Look under the alphabetical country listing in the Yahooligans Around the World Directory at
    http://www.yahooligans.com/Around_the_World/Countries
Choose the part of the world you're interested in, then scroll down to choose the country using the
    Geographia Web Site at
    http://www.geographia.com
Use the drop-down menus to either choose the region or country at the Lonely Planet Destinations
    section at
    http://www.lonelyplanet.com/destinations/

Maldives
Ngcheong-Lum, Roseline. *Maldives (Cultures of the World)*. Tarrytown, NY: Marshall Cavendish, 2000.

Oman
Allen, Calvin H. *Oman (Creation of the Modern Middle East)*. Philadelphia, PA: Chelsea House
    Publications, 2002.
Barnett, Tracy L. *Oman*. Broomall, PA: Mason Crest Publishers, 2003.
Foster, Leila Merrell. *Oman (Enchantment of the World)*. New York: Children's Press, 1999.
Isaac, Michael. *Historical Atlas of Oman*. New York: Rosen Publishing Group, 2004.

Pakistan
Aykroyd, Clarissa. *Pakistan: The Growth and Influence of Islam in the Nations of Asia and Central Asia*.
    Broomall, PA: Mason Crest Publishers, 2005.
Crompton, Samuel Willard. *Pakistan (Major World Nations)*. Philadelphia, PA: Chelsea House
    Publications, 2002.
DeAngelis, Gina. *Pakistan (Many Cultures, One World)*. Mankato, MN: Blue Earth Books, 2003.
Graham, Ian. *Pakistan (Country Files)*. North Mankato, MN: Smart Apple Media, 2003.
Greenberger, Robert. *A Historical Atlas of Pakistan*. New York: Rosen Publishing Group, 2003.
Heinrichs, Ann. *Pakistan (True Books)*. Chicago, IL: Children's Press, 2005.
Kwek, Karen, and Jameel Hague. *Welcome to Pakistan (Welcome to My Country)*. Milwaukee, WI:
    Gareth Stevens Publishing, 2003.
Sharth, Sharon. *Pakistan (Countries: Faces and Places)*. Chanhassen, MN: Child's World, 2003.
Sheehan, Sean. *Pakistan (Cultures of the World)*. Tarrytown, NY: Marshall Cavendish, 2005.
Taus-Bolstad, Stacy. *Pakistan in Pictures (Visual Geography Series)*. Minneapolis, MN: Lerner
    Publications, 2003.

Index

abaya, 303
Addu Atoll, Maldives, 291
Afghans in Pakistan, 318, 319, 328, 342
Africans: in the Maldives, 292; in Oman, 302–3
Ahmad bin Said, Sultan of Oman, 299
Akbar the Great, Emperor, 317, 318
Alexander the Great, 315
Al-Hajar Mountains, Oman, 309
Andre, Andreas, 290–91
Arabic: in the Maldives, 295; in Oman, 303–4, 310
Arabs: in the Maldives, 292; in Oman, 298, 299, 302; in Pakistan, 316–17
architecture: in Oman, 306; in Pakistan, 318, *318*
art in Pakistan, *314*, 316, *316*, 318
Aryans in Pakistan, 314–15, 325–27
Asoka, Emperor, 315
Aurangzeb, Emperor, 317
ayyalah, 311
Aziz, Shaukat, 323

Baa Atoll, Maldives, 295
Baba, Abdul Rahman, 340
Bābur, Emperor, 317
bagh, 341
Bagri, 325
Bahawalpur, Pakistan, 342
Bahlā', Oman, *300*
Bakhsh, Data Ganj, 332
Balti, 331
Baluchi people, 327–28, *327*, 341–42
Baluchistan, Pakistan, 317, 327–28, *327*, 334
Bangladesh, 321, *321*, 322, 324
Bangladeshis in Oman, 302–3
Barakat, Sultan Abu Al, 290
Basant, 343, *343*
Bedouin in Oman, 306, 310–11
bhangra, 340
Bhitai, Shah Abdul Latif, 340
Bhutto, Benazir, 321–22
Bhutto, Zulfikar Ali, 321
Birir, Pakistan, 329
biryani, 337
bodu beru, 295
boti kebab, 337
Brahui, 328
British Empire, 291–92, 318–19
Buddhists, 293, 315, *315*, 316, 333
bull butting, 311
Bumboret, Pakistan, 329
burka, 303, *306*, 326
Burushkashi, 330, 339
Burusho, 330
buzkashi, 342

carpet making, 341–42
chapati, 336

child labor in Pakistan, *324*, 333, *333*
Chitralis, 330
Cholistan, Pakistan, 342
Christians, 304, 332
churidars, 326
clothing: in Oman, 303, *303*, *306*; in Pakistan, 323, 326, *326*, 341
crafts: in the Maldives, 295; in Oman, 310–11; in Pakistan, 331, 341–42, *341*
cricket, 342

dahi, 337
dal, 337, *337*
dance: in the Maldives, 295; in Oman, 311; in Pakistan, 340, *340*
Dari, 328
Darius I, King of Persia, 315
Darra Adam Khel, Pakistan, 328
Demetrius, King, 315–16
Dhatki, 325
Dhivehi language, 292–93
Dhivehi people, 292
Dhofar, Oman, 299, 301, 304, 306
dhol, 340
dholak, 339
Didi, Amin, 291
Dir, Pakistan, 328
dishdasha, 303, *303*
Dravidians in the Maldives, 292
dupiatta, *323*, 326

education: in the Maldives, 295, *295*; in Oman, *304*, 310; in Pakistan, 338–39
Egyptians in Oman, 303
Eid ul-Adha, 305
Eid ul-Fitr, 305, 343
English language: in the Maldives, 293; in Oman, 310; in Pakistan, 323, 335

Faisal bin Turki, Sultan of Oman, 299–300
falconry, 311
fandita, 293
farming: in the Maldives, 294; in Oman, 306, 307–8; in Pakistan, 329, *333*, 334
Farsi, 328
festivals: in the Maldives, 293; in Oman, 305; in Pakistan, 343, *343*
Filipinos in Oman, 303
fishing: in the Maldives, 295; in Pakistan, 334
food and drink: in the Maldives, 294; in Oman, 308–9, *308*; in Pakistan, 336–38, *336*, *337*
frankincense, 297, 298, *298*, 306

Gandhara, 316
Gayoom, Maumoon Abdul, 292
ghazal, 339
ghee, *336*
Gilgit, Pakistan, 330, 331

Gojal, Pakistan, 332
Gujar, 331
Gujarati, 327
Gurjaras, 316

halvah, *308*, 309
Haqq, Talib al-, 298
Harappa, Pakistan, 314
Hazara, 328
health care: in the Maldives, 294–95; in Oman, 309–10, *309*; in Pakistan, 338
Hindus, 304, 315, 324, 332–33
housing: in the Maldives, 294; in Oman, *305*, 306; in Pakistan, 329, *329*, 330, 335
Hunza, Pakistan, *312*, 332
Hunzai, Allamah Nasir al-Din Nasir, *339*
Hussain, Shah, 343
Huvadhu Atoll, Maldives, 291
Hyderabad, Pakistan, 319, 325

Ibad, Abdullah bin, 299
Ibadis, 299, 304
Indians: in the Maldives, 291, 292, 293; in Oman, 302–3, 304
industry: in the Maldives, 294; in Oman, 308; in Pakistan, 334
Indus Valley, Pakistan, 313–14, 315, 319, 333, 334
Iqbal, Sir Muhammad, 320
Iranians in Oman, 304
Iraqis in Oman, 304
Islamabad, Pakistan, 325, 334, 335–36
Ismaili Muslims, 330, 332

Jabalis, 302
jalfrezi, 337
Jammu and Kashmir, Pakistan. *See* Kashmir
Jashen Bahran, 343, *343*
Jinnah, Mohammed Ali, 320, *320*, 326
Jofari, 306
Jordanians in Oman, 303

kabaddi, 343
Kalamis, 330
Kalasha people, 326, 329, *329*
Kalat, Pakistan, 328, 334
kameez, 326, *326*
kandoura, 303
Kanishka, 316
Karachi, Pakistan, 324, 325, 333, 334, *334*, 335, *335*, 336
karai, 337
Karakoram Mountains, Pakistan, 330
Karimabad, Pakistan, *312*
Kashmir, Pakistan, 320, 322, 331, *331*
keer, 337
Khan, Gulam Ishaq, 321
Khan, Hashim, 342

Page numbers in *italic* indicate illustrations.

Khan, Imran, 342
Khan, Jahangir, 342
Khan, Liaquat Ali, 320
Khan, Mohammad Ayub, 320
Khan, Nusrat Fateh Ali, 339
Khan, Yahya, 320–21
khanjar, 310, *310*, 311
Khosrow, Amir, 332
Kipling, Rudyard, 335
Koli, 325
Kuda Id, 293
kulfi, 337
kumma, 303, *303*
kurta, 326
Kushan people, 316

laban, 309
Lahore, Pakistan, 318, *318*, 325, *332*, 334, 335, 336, *338*, *342*, 343, *343*
Lailat ul-Miraj, 305
languages: in the Maldives, 292–93, 295; in Oman, 303–4, 310; in Pakistan, 323–25, 327, 328, 329, 330, 331, 335, 339
Lasi, 328
lassi, 338
literature in Pakistan, 339–40, *339*
liwa, 311

Mahmud of Ghaznī, 317
makhbousa, 308
Male, Maldives, *291*, 293–94, *293*
Mangan Empire, 297
maqudeed, 308
Masqat, Oman, 299, *301*, 304, 305, *311*
massar, 303
Maṭraḥ, Oman, 305, *305*
Mauryan Empire, 315
Mela Cheraghan, 343
Menander (Milinda), King, 316
Mirza, Iskandar, 320
Mohajir, 324
Mohenjo Daro, Pakistan, 314
moutabel, 308
Mughal Empire, 317–18
Muhammad bin Qasim, 317
Muhammad of Ghor, 317
Muinuddheen II, Sultan Muhammad, 291
Multan, Pakistan, *325*, 341, 342
Musandam Peninsula, Oman, 306
Musharraf, Pervez, 322–23, 324
music: in the Maldives, 295; in Oman, 311, *311*; in Pakistan, 332, 339, 340
Muslims: in the Maldives, 290, 293, *293*; in Oman, 298, 299, 303–4, *304*, 305; in Pakistan, 316–17, *318*, 330, 331–32, *332*, 340, 343

naan, 336
na'ashat, 311
Napier, Sir Charles, 319
Nasir, Ibrahim, 291, 292

Nawabshah, Pakistan, 325
Nilandhe Atoll, Maldives, 295
nomads, 306, 327, 328
North-West Frontier Province (NWFP), Pakistan, 319, 328–31, *328*, 342
Nur Jahan, 318

Od, 325
oil industry, 301, 308
oud, 311, *311*

pakora, 338
Palestinians in Oman, 303
paratha, 336, *336*
Parsis, 333
Parthians, 316
Pashtun, 326, 328, *328*, 330, 340
Persian Empire, 298, 315
Peshawar, Pakistan, 316, 328, 334, 336, *337*, *341*
phulkari, 341
pilaf, 308, 337
polo, 342, *342*
Porus, King, 315
poverty in Pakistan, *324*, 325, 333
Punjab, Pakistan, 314, 315, 317, 318, 319, *319*, 325–27, *325*, *333*, 341, 343
Punjabi people, 325–27, 340
puri, 336

qabooli, 308
Qaboos bin Said, Sultan of Oman, 301–2, *302*, 305, 306, 309
qahwa, 309
qaum, 327
qawwali, 332, 339, 340, 343
Quetta, Pakistan, 327, 328, 334, 336

raa, 294
Rahman, Sheikh Mujibur, 321
Rajasthani, 327
Ramadan, 305, 343
Ravahe, 292
religions: in the Maldives, 293, *293*; in Oman, 304–5, *304*; in Pakistan, 329, 330, 331–33, *332*, 343
roti, 336
rukhal, 308
Rumbur, Pakistan, 329
Ruwī, Oman, 305

sadha chaval, 337
Said bin Taimur, Sultan of Oman, 300–301
Saif, Imam Sultan bin, 299
Saka, 316
Saleh, Imam Isa bin, 300
salwar, 326, *326*
samosa, 338
Sanāw, Oman, *303*
Sānghar, Pakistan, 325
Sansi, 325
Saraiki, 327

Sayyid Said bin Sultan, Sultan of Oman, 299
Seleucus I, King of Persia, 315
Shah, Bulleh, 340
Shah Jahan, Emperor, 317, *317*, 318
Sharif, Nawaz, 321, 322
sherwani, 326
Shia Muslims: in the Maldives, 293; in Oman, 304; in Pakistan, 332
Shikarpur, Pakistan, 325
Shina, 331
shuwa, 308
Sikhs in Pakistan, 318, 319, 333
Sind, Pakistan, 314, 315, 317, 318, 319, 324–25, *324*, 327, 328, 341
Sindhi language, 324–25, 327
Sindhi people, 324–25
Singh, Ranjit, 318
sirwal, 303
soccer, 295
South Maalhosmadulu Atoll, Maldives, 295
sports: in the Maldives, 295; in Oman, 307, 311; in Pakistan, 342–43, *342*
squash, 342
Sri Lankans: in the Maldives, 292, 293; in Oman, 302–3
Sufis, 332, 339, 340, 343
Ṣuḥār, Oman, 299
Sukkur, Pakistan, 325
Sunni muslims: in the Maldives, 293; in Oman, 304; in Pakistan, 332
Sūr, Oman, 304
Swat, Pakistan, 330
Syrians in Oman, 303

tabla, 339
Taimur, Sultan of Oman, 200
tamboura, 311
Taxila, Pakistan, 315, *315*, 316
Temür (Tamerlane), 317
Thakurufaan, Muhammad, 291
Thanaa, 292–93
Thar Desert, Pakistan, 325
Tharparkar, Pakistan, 325
tonga, 335
Torwalis, 330
tourism in the Maldives, 294, *294*, 295

Urdu, 323–24, 327, 335, 339

Wagah, Pakistan, 322, *322*
Wahibas, 302
Wakhi, 330
Waneci, 328
White Huns, 316
wizar, 303
women in society: in the Maldives, 293; in Oman, 307, *307*; in Pakistan, 326, 330, 338

zatar, 309
Zia-Ul-Haq, Muhammad, 321

Page numbers in *italic* indicate illustrations.